Against the Wind

A Memoir

Mary E. Matury Gibson

STRATTON
PRESS
Publishing Life

Against the Wind

Stratton Press Publishing
831 N Tatnall Street Suite M #188,
Wilmington, DE 19801
www.stratton-press.com
1-888-323-7009

ISBN (Paperback): 978-1-64895-038-4
ISBN (Ebook): 978-1-64895-039-1

Printed in the United States of America

DEDICATED TO THE ONES I LOVE

Forward

In a place somewhere, perhaps it is just down the street, a voice cries out for help. Perhaps it is an old woman or man with wrinkled skin, white hair and sad eyes. Will help come?

There is a man in a wheelchair trying to cross the street, will help come to him? Maybe he is dirty, in need of a bath. He is trying to balance a small grocery bag on his lap as he crosses a busy intersection. He is missing a right leg. There is a bottle of cheap wine sticking out of the bag on his lap. Will aid come to him?

In the dark of night I have awakened to the cry of someone in pain. I was sure I heard it. I sit up and look around, I hear no such cry. I lie back down and try to sleep but the memory of that cry lingers on in my head. How can we know another's pain? Because we have suffered pain ourselves at one time. Remembering such pain and the knowledge of what it is to want it gone, to be whole again and healthy, can be a powerful force. It can drive the desire to help another even when it is not convenient or the one in need looks unsavory, not the right kind.

Help others; raise them up from their despair and need. In doing so, one will rise even higher. To look down on those who are down, in pain and suffering, is to be brought down with them.

Chapter 1

Lonely Has A Face

It is 6:30 A.M. I'm up. It's a bright sunny morning with the smell of an approaching autumn in the air. There is a tree with yellow leaves just outside my second floor condo. It is splashing a beautiful yellow light onto the Maplewood floor of my living room. Somewhere in the distance a bird is singing. As I look around me I know I have no reason to be sad, angry or depressed about anything. This indeed is a day which God has made.

I don't live in the lap of luxury by any standards, but I feel I live well. My three bedroom two bath condo has served me well these last ten years. It faces the golf course from the other side of a small pond. The geese are here this morning. They were up very early. I heard them about five o'clock. The nine holes course and the rest of the grounds are surrounded by big trees of oak, evergreen, weeping willow and maple. I can't see or hear the traffic from the street. Occasionally I will hear a golfer yell "Four!"

I guess, for a girl born on a farm to immigrant parents who came through Ellis Island in 1929, I've done alright for myself. Back then I had to share a bed with as many as three siblings at one time. I was the last of six to leave home. I really can't call myself a girl anymore now that I'm over sixty-five and headed for retirement, although I still feel like a kid. Being the youngest child always made it hard for me to feel like an adult. My siblings always considered me a child and, therefore, in their eyes I've never really grown up. I'm the only one of the six children my parents had that has a college degree. I also make more money than any of them, but I'm still, interestingly enough, looked upon as a poor halfwit by my surviving brothers. I think they feel justified in this attitude due to the fact they were always considered first and more important than the females of the family.

The air is crisp as I leave my sanctuary to start my day. In the car the CD player is blasting, Jerry Lee Lewis singing "The news is out all over town...........!" I need this music to help me get going in the morning, along with a strong cup of Joe. I feel gloomy as I think I know news that is not out all over town. I fear it will never be unless I try to tell it. So I will get on with the telling of this tale to the best of my ability.

I pull into the parking lot an hour later. This is called a Nursing and Rehab Center. I beg to differ with this name as I don't see much nursing or rehab going on here. There is a car coming in the opposite direction. I have my turn signal on and indicate with a wave of hand out the window I want to pull into the spot on my left. The other car approaching stops next to mine as the driver shakes her head "no". I drive on as she takes the parking spot. This is a fight I don't care to take on this morning. I have many more important battles to face in this hell hole of a nursing and rehab center for the elderly and infirmed. It is energy wasted!

I find a spot on the other side of the building. As I get out of my car it is already very warm. A hot white sun beats down on me. I walk to the entrance of the nursing home. A breeze is blowing but it stops me in my tracks. I smell urine and feces as well as human sweat, bacon, eggs, maple syrup, coffee and the heat of the day. My brief case feels very heavy in my right hand as I open the door with my left and enter.

I'm tired and feel defeated already. I remind myself that I do meaningful work. I'm lucky to have any job in these economic hard times. Many are not as fortunate. I know this America is not my fathers and his band of relatives who came here and made a better life for us. America struggles now and we must all struggle with her. The best way to wait out a bad economy is to keep working and spend less. I am happy that I can still work after battling cancer twice, having a minor stroke, and coping with high blood pressure and diabetes. I pull myself together now and put on a happy face.

Lola ignores me as I approach the front desk. She's on the phone talking to someone about last night's party. The conversation is personal, not related to nursing home business. I steady my nerves by telling myself it is not her fault that she's poorly trained and doesn't take her job seriously. I tell myself it's hard for her when I'm sure she is getting paid barely minimum wage.

In about ten minutes she finishes her personal call. All lines on her board are now lit up like a down town Christmas tree. She continues to ignore me. At the first opportunity I say "Good morning Lola. May I have my patient list please?" I say it fast before she has a chance to answer another call and put me off again. She gives me a dead pan look and tries to print the list from her desk top. After fifteen more minutes of her trying, I go to the office next door and ask again for the list. I finally secure it.

I start down the long hallway. Dust particles are dancing in the sunlight streaming in the big windows. Wheelchairs are lined up all along the corridor as closed to the sunny windows as possible. There is a sea of white hair and faces filled with questioning looks. As I glance at each one of them they seem to be saying "Are you here for me? Are you here for me? Are you here for me?"

The heat is on, even though the temperature outdoors is now approaching eighty-five degrees. There is no air moving anywhere in the building. I feel the sweat begin to trickle down my back as I try to negotiate the hallway where many old and wrinkled hands are reaching for me. Some of the people are calling "Help Me! Help Me!" Others call out my name. I think, yes, lonely has a face. It is the face of neglect, the face of wanting, of wanting anything, a touch, a kind word, a plea. It is a longing for release from the loneliness and pain that is so present in all of their eyes that you can almost touch it.

I make my way to the first unit. I pass Arlene the Screamer. She is quiet today as she sits in her wheelchair. She has long gray hair with silvery white highlights. Someone has put it back into a pony tail.

Her skin is very white, almost transparent. She is quite thin. She is very delicate. I know she was very beautiful in her day. Hanging from her chair is an 8X10 black and white photo of her on her wedding day. She is wearing a magnificent full length gown of the day. Most likely it was 1940 or 1945. I can see it as I pass by her, that lovely young woman. Then I stop and look up into Arlene's eyes which are brilliant blue. They dance and smile at me. The years seem to fade away as I see the soul of the younger woman as she once was, vibrant and happy with so much to give the world. The old woman sitting there has gone as I gaze into her eyes, captivated. I say a small prayer in my head as she clings to my hand. "My God My God, why have you forsaken her?"

A nurse is yelling my name, pulling me out of my reverie. I let go of Arlene's hand and move on. "Josephine won't take her meds. She spit them at me." She says as I come closer. The nurse is not one I would call a good caring nurse. Josephine is shouting and flailing her arms in the air.

I move in close to her and start singing a few lines, "Amazing Grace how sweet the sound, that saved a retch like me " As I sing, Josephine begins to calm down. She hasn't eaten any of her breakfast. I ask the nurse for another dose of her pills. Jo continues to hold my hand and sway in her chair to the imaginary strains of the song that still lingers in the air. There is a thick strawberry shake on her tray. It is about four ounces. I mix her crushed meds into it and give it to her. I talk to her in a soft low toned voice about how nice she looks in her red top and red pants. The drink is gone in a flash. I request another which she drinks without difficulty. The nurse looks on with expression of total dislike for the old woman who just had her ninety-seventh birthday and me.

I sit at the nurse's station and write orders for her. I know the chance of them actually doing what I ask is slim to none. Order: "Please crush meds and give them to patient in a thick shake daily." I leave the desk area and start my journey down another hallway. There are many patients here for me to see. I will have to pick up speed so I don't get behind.

Alice is just coming from rehab when I reach her room. She has tears in her eyes. I ask her what's wrong. "My leg is killing me. I can't stand the pain anymore." She holds out a plump right leg for me to look at. I run my fingers along the inside of the brace on it that extends from her thigh to her ankle. There at the ankle I can't get my fingers under the brace. She moans and I look up at her.

"The brace is too tight and it is cutting her at the ankle!" I say to the therapist. "Alice is this where it hurts you?" she nods in silence as the tears run down her face.

"Yeah, she's gitten a new one in a few days." The therapist says in a voice that expresses how uninterested he is in what I'm telling him. His name tag reads "Gregg P.T." I'm on my knees next to Alice's wheelchair.

"But it hurts her now," I reply. "Please place some padding between the brace and the ankle." On my way out of this rehab unit I return to check Alice's ankle again. There is no padding there and she is still crying in pain. I get the padding and do it myself. When I look up I see the therapist standing in the door way looking at me with such hate and distain that it could have stopped a speeding train. I got Alice a pain pill and wrote some orders for staff to check the brace every shift and make sure the padding is in place until she can get fitted for the new brace. I know I should have talked to that therapist again. I just don't have the time or the patience for those who are so uninterested in doing their jobs as health care providers. I take the simple way out and just do it myself.

As the smell of lunch cooking , beef stew and more urine and feces, begins to fill the stifling hot air, I'm about to finish my rounds. Sweat has now stained the back of my blouse and neck as well. Beads of perspiration formed on my upper lip. The Nigerian nurse looks up from her desk and takes in the sight of me. "I don't foe the life ah me know why you wear them fancy assed clothes to come here and see these old folks, Miss Mary." She is pretty nice. She makes an effort to help me and the residents here on the ward. I know her English as well as her education are very limited. But I wonder to myself if this is the best we have to offer these who have given the world their whole lives? This center is supposed to be one of the better ones in the state! It is located in a fairly affluent neighborhood.

"I likes Miss Mary's beautiful and bright colored clothes!" yells Blind Susie from her perch across from the nurse's desk. I look up in her direction as she has snapped me out of my musing.

"You blind!" exclaims the nurse. "How you know what she look like?"

"Oh I knows, I knows" says Susie. "Just cause I'm blind don't mean I can't see color and smell when Miss Mary is a comin. Her perfume and clothes light up my day."

I can't say a thing or I'll start crying. But I guess it is what makes me keep coming back here day after hot, sticky, smelly, fuming day. It is now noon; I give Susie's shoulder a rub as I pass by her on my way to the lobby. She pats my hand.

Jason, the janitor, is mopping the lobby as I walk to the door. He stops and leans on his mop giving me a big smile with many teeth missing. "I like yo pretty outfit you got on t'day Miss Mary." He says to me.

"Thank you Jason" I reply. "I'm glad you like it." I know that I probably over dress for the type of work I do. But I know it brings a little pleasure to both the residents and the occasional staff member.

Most might be offended to be called by their first name by staff and residents but I like it. I always ask them to address me that way. I don't like to be called "Doctor." I'm not a doctor at all. I'm a Nurse Practitioner. I've never been crazy about that title either, so I find that Mary or Miss Mary is just fine with me. "Nurse Mary" or "Mary the Nurse" is also ok with me. When I was in the Army, I addressed my superiors as" General" or "Cornel" and they always referred to me as "Mary". Although I had achieved the rank of captain; I somehow was called by my first name. When I began to work in the hospital as a young nurse, it was proper etiquette to address the physician as Doctor along with their last name. All nurses were Miss or Mrs. Whomever. I was always called just "Mary".

There isn't a day that goes by that I don't have to explain to someone what a Nurse Practitioner is and what it is that we do. I know of no other profession that has to do it day in and day out. The

Doctors don't understand the role. I must explain it to them as well. I have my little spiel down so well that it sounds like I'm reading it out of a book.

It goes like this. "A Nurse Practitioner is a nurse with an advanced degree in nursing who is educated to diagnose and treat all kinds of illnesses and injuries. He/she may order tests and prescribe medications as needed by the patient in collaboration with doctors and other health care providers. The Nurse practitioner may also review the results of these tests and interpret them for the patient. The Nurse Practitioner does not require direct supervision by a doctor. A collaborative agreement with a physician is all that is required in this state."

About half way into the spiel the reply would be, "Why don't you just become a doctor if that's what you want to do?"

Then I must explain that doctors are busy people and most only have time to focus on treatment of the person's present illness. The Nurse Practitioner, however, looks at the patient as a whole person. She must gather much information, such as, what is the family like? What type of work does the patient do? What do they know about wellness and illness? What do they need to know to take care of themselves and their loved ones etc. By that time, whomever I'm talking to is uninterested. That person has moved on or is now staring at me with glassy eyes of either disbelief, pure boredom or both.

As a young nurse, I worked in the hospital where I thought I would remain until I died. After receiving an advanced degree, I've spent the last thirty years working as a Nurse Practitioner. Half my day is spent explaining what it is that I do and the other half trying to do it. Now that I am approaching almost fifty year as a nurse, I'm grateful for having had the privilege and the honor of having cared for so many. I have had the opportunity to earn a decent living in order to raise my children. As I near my retirement, I find myself here among the most unfortunate members of our society who need much more than I can possibly give them. Lonely is the face of the forgotten people. Perhaps by shedding some light on their pain and suffering I may help them more than any pill I can give them. Come and journey with me among those who have no voice in great American society.

Chapter 2

The Fine Line Between Sane And Insane

The next place, Whispering Pines, is the worst one I have to visit in order to take care of those who are unable to provide for themselves. You may get the joke as I make my way around the place. I get out of the car and start walking across the drive way. I'm in the middle of it when a bus flies in and almost runs me over as it pulls up to the front door and stops. The driver gets out.

"You almost hit me!" I exclaim, a little breathlessly.

He looks at me and replies "So who the hell are you? Git yo fat ass outta my way or git hit. I got ta git these here patients to the day program and I'm late!" I turn and walk inside in order to avoid further argument clearly going nowhere. I set the alarm off as always happened when I come in. The front desk person is on the phone and ignores the sound. It is extremely loud and sounds like there is a fire in the building. It seems to faze no one but me.

"Please turn it off!" I shout as loud as I can over the noise. The receptionist lifts her foot to a switch on the desk and flips it. The deafening noise stops. The alarm is a necessary evil here. It is to alert the staff to an elopement. That's a fancy way of saying someone is trying to escape.

Inside it is somewhat like the movie "Snake Pit," only worse. The noise is almost unbearable. There's yelling and swearing like one would never hear anywhere else. There are not a lot of elderly people here. The residents are all psychiatric patients who would otherwise be living in the street or under a viaduct if such facilities didn't exist. Thanks to the Nursing Home and institutional Act of 1972, these people have nowhere else to go. This act sought to prevent people from being institutionalized for years or for life thus becoming unable to function in society. The rules and norms of behavior of the institution became a way of life before the act was put into effect. One of the administrators of a large mental institution was an instructor of mine in nursing school. She was one of the coauthors' of the bill. She had an epiphany one day as she walked through the grounds of the institution where she worked. It was located on large parcels of land set off from the rest of the community so interaction between the place and the community never existed. "One morning as I was walking to my office, I began to notice what was going on around me," she told her class of eager nursing students. "As I walked through the large park that extended around two side of the large building on a bright sunny morning, I saw a couple engaging in sexual intercourse. They were right there on a bench next to the side walk totally naked. They didn't seem to care or take note of anyone else who was passing. It was not the first time I had seen this but it was the first time that it really started to bother me. When I entered the building, a resident of the institution was defecating and smearing his feces on the wall next to the entrance. Another man was standing next to a large pot of artificial flowers. He had no pants on, only a shirt and he was urinating into the fake flowers. When I walked down the hallway to my office, I saw two kitchen aides smoking next to the cart that contained breakfast trays for the residents. They lifted the lids off two of the trays and proceeded to put out their cigarettes in the food on the plates. I passed a topless woman as I walked into my office. I felt strange and uncomfortable. I couldn't sit down at my desk so I just stood there staring out the window. What was wrong with me? I began to ask myself. None of this ever bothered me before. I had been the chief administrator there for fifteen years. I had seen every bizarre thing there was to see. Then I began to realize that was it. What bothered me most was that over the years I had come to accept this behavior as normal and did nothing to correct it or improve the conditions of the staff and residents in my care. In the act of accepting this antisocial behavior, I and everyone around me had become institutionalized. I knew I needed to do something about it."

While this act, in theory, was a good idea, in reality, it has had many ill effects on patients and society as a whole. It basically stated a person could not be held in an institution indefinitely if that person did not voluntarily want to be there. Reasons for admittance and time limits on stays were instituted. No one foresaw the impact of spewing all these people into the community at large. There was no plan in place, no means of housing and supporting them as most are too ill to care for themselves. They couldn't function or hold even the most basic job. So the only alternative was to place them in nursing homes. I can guarantee that you don't want any of them to be flipping your burger or making your favorite latté'. The ages of the "residents", as they are called, is young adult through old age.

A blue haze is in the air as the pungent odor of smoke hits me hard. I cough and my eyes are watering badly. There is also the smell of food and human sweat, feces and urine. I can see excrement and pools of dark yellow urine on the floor. I avoid them. Across from the nurse's station there is a water fountain. Elmer is standing by it with his pants down urinating into it. I alert the nurse and the janitor who is mopping the floor nearby. They are both oblivious to what is going on. The nurse yells at Elmer to stop and the janitor throws some disinfectant at the fountain that makes me choke. They both walk away. Red faced with tears streaming down, I cough and move away from the area.

I have made it my policy to never eat, drink or use the bathroom in any of these facilities. Even taking a deep cleansing breath is not an option on most days. I don't ever touch my face or my clothes while I'm here. I constantly wash my hands to I keep well while trying my best to attend to the needs of the staff and the patients.

Yes, the staff too. If they have a cold, an eye infection or a rash I give them meds. While I try to be as thorough as I can, hallway medicine is never a good thing. All practitioners do it. People who work in these places have little money and no health insurance, so I try to help them. If they take off work, they may lose the job or leave the place too short staffed. Some staff, even poorly educated, is better than none at all. It is the philosophy of most of these God forsaken places.

I like most of the people that work here, believe it or not! They are the most uneducated staff of all the facilities I visit. Many are good people in their hearts. They want to learn and do the right thing for the patients. I see Mrs. Martin at the nurse's station. She has a heart of gold. She is a Licensed Practical Nurse with little real education; however, she tries her best every day. She asks questions and expresses an interest in understanding why I give certain meds and request specific tests for the patients.

Mrs. Martin has type II diabetes and I have tried to teach her to eat better. She holds up a bottle of water for me to see. "Look Miss Mary!" she calls out "No more pop!" I give her thumbs up and smile.

Moving down the hallway, I try to go to as many of the patients on my list as I can. I usually get about ten or so seen at a time. The hallways are crowded with residents today. Some of them are engaged in activities best done behind closed doors. They are close to engaging in public fornication. Ulla Lee is one of them. She waves me away and says "Can you come back later when I not so busy?" She has no income only the thirty dollars a month the home allows each resident to keep out of there state aid checks. Solicitation is her way to get spending money for her makeup, smokes and snack foods. I want her to quit smoking but I haven't come up with a good plan yet to get her to stop. Since this is her home, I can't interfere in her extra-curricular activities either. She is a consenting adult and, therefore, she can engage in this type of activity. I just wish she would confine it to her room. I also know it's her way of advertising her services as well.

It is a well-known fact psyche patients are much easier to deal with and control their behavior if they smoke. Some meds do produce a boost in brain chemistry that helps them; however, the effects are not long lasting. The meds are expensive and the patients often don't like the side effects and refuse to take them. I've never seen a psyche patient turn down a smoke even if they can't breathe due to asthma and emphysema. Schizophrenia and bipolar disorder are difficult to control in a population that lacks basic education and reasoning skills. The well brought up and better educated who have these diseases fare much better than the poor with these same ailments.

As I move on, Kenny is standing at the end of the hall by the smoke room. He is talking to himself, as usual, using language that is unfit for human ears. He is "mother fucking" someone I can't see. He is probably the sickest and most dangerous of all the residents. He is not my patient, thank God! But I have no fear of him because he likes me. "Hi Kenny," I call out to him. He immediately stops the string of profanities in mid-sentence. His face changes to a bright white toothed smile. He is a handsome black man of about thirty-five years old. He is always well dressed. Today he is wearing a pair of designer men's shorts and a T-shirt of bright yellow.

"Miss Mary," he says, "I'm so glad to see you. How is your partner, Leda, today?" Kenny is obsessed with Leda as most men his age would be. She is a young new nurse practitioner who never seems to have a top that fits. Her large white breasts are always hanging over the low cut neck lines she wears. I don't think any man has ever looked at her face, although she is quite beautiful, they are always looking at her chest. She is a pretty blonde girl who has absolutely no idea what she is doing. I brought her here once to show her around because the boss asked me to do it. Kenny has seen her only that one time and it has left a lasting impression.

"Leda is doing fine, Kenny" I tell him with a smile as I continue walking down the hallway.

Oh no! Here comes the nursing supervisor and her assistant. They're both a pain in my side! Ok, well maybe that pain is a little lower. "Miss Mary," whines the super. "Can't you use your influence and get us some post-operative patients in here that need rehab and wound care? You know, like some old ladies with fractured hips and knee replacements."

"You know I can't do that Ms. Brown. I can't until you change some of the policies that I have already outlined for you. Those changes need to happen before it is safe to place those who are unable to defend themselves in this facility." I reply as politely as I can.

A woman was placed here once who needed wound care. She woke in the middle of the night with Elmer, Mr. Pee in the water fountain himself, trying to get in bed with her. "I screamed for over an hour, Miss Mary, I was so terrified, before someone came in to get him off me. Please, I beg of you, get me out of here!" the family had her transferred to another facility the very next day. I couldn't bring myself to persuade them to keep her here. I would have done the same and more had it been my loved one.

"Mona, have you gotten an IV into Mr. Moore yet?" I ask the assistant, in an attempt to change the subject. I needed information on Mr. Moore as well. He has been waiting five days for someone to get an IV line into him so he can receive antibiotic for a serious infection called C-Dif.

"No one can start it, Miss Mary, even the IV company has been here and can't do It." she replies. I'm mad now and can feel my face getting red. The poor man has been here for five days waiting for the IV administration of drugs to help him survive a bad infection that could take his life. No one is worried that he hasn't gotten this life saving treatment. The home had agreed to supply it when they accepted the patient into the facility for care.

"Don't make me come down there and start that IV" I threaten. They know I really shouldn't do it because a provider is not an employee of the facility and cannot provide direct nursing care. Dr. Big Guy, my boss, would never concern himself. Most Doctors are not good at starting IVs anyway, unless they're an anesthesiologist. We are also not covered by insurance in such instances.

"Well you wouldn't get it either" she retorts. Now I'm really mad.

"Get me the stuff and meet me in Mr. Moore's room, now please!" I demand. Five minutes later I stick Mr. Moore one time and the IV is in. Mona is standing behind me. "Here you can clean it now and dress it for him". I walk to the sink and start scrubbing my hands. At the desk, I write more orders that I can only hope will get done in a week or two.

Mona approaches the desk with tears in her eyes "Just cause you old and can do all this here kinda stuff don't allow you to be so mean to me," she says. I know where this is going. It is going straight to my boss. I will surely get another lecture on being nice to the staff.

It's getting late and I have seen at least twenty patients so far today. It's two in the afternoon and I'm late for my office hours. I turn and give Mona a big hug and an apology for my bad behavior. I know it is not her fault. There is some truth in what she has just said. I am old and I do have more skill. I have too much responsibility and no authority to change anything or make it better. I can't hire or fire the staff or demand they hire better educated nurses. They will not spend the money, nor will good nurses want to work in a facility where the standard of care is so low.

I pass Elmer in the hallway as he is smearing his feces on the wall. No one is stopping him or seems concerned. Whispering Pines indeed! What an oxymoron.

I head for the parking lot where I find Kenny standing next to my car. There is no security officer at the facility even though it is one of the most dangerous. The profanity is streaming from him in a deep, fevered, sinister type voice, like a fulminating witches cauldron. Kenny's face is twisted in anger. His large black biceps are glistening in the high afternoon sun. My eyes trace down to his slim waist making that beautiful V shaped body that all young men wish to sport. Yes, Kenny has it all; too bad he is so sick and cannot function in society. I wait. He sees me now and his face changes immediately to that bright handsome smile. "Miss Mary, how is this old hog runnin?" He asks as he kicks the left front tire of my old town car.

"Oh it's running just fine now, Kenny." I reply, opening the door and placing my brief case on the front seat. I turn and he is now standing between me and my open car door. It's not a good move on my part. He could twist me like a pretzel and snap my neck like a twig in two seconds. He could take my car and be gone. No one would find me until the change of shifts, if at all. The residents who wander the grounds are oblivious to others. So much for preventing institutional behavior, I guess.

"You know, I had me a Mustang once and I loved that car, it ran like a top and I was cool in it." He said in a pleasant voice. I remind myself that he likes me and he especially likes Leda. I have always treated him as if he is perfectly normal, sort of like a neighbor I would talk to over the back fence.

"Well I love this car; it's such a nice ride. I'm not sure I could get another like it anymore, it's so old. You know they just don't make them like they used to either." I say calmly as I look at my watch. "Well Kenny, I've got to get to the office." He hesitates, never taking his big brown eyes off me for an instant. He slowly moves out from my open door. I let out a slow deep breath of relief that I hope is not detected by him.

"You say Hi to Leda for me won't you?" He asks with a sad look on his face.

"Of course I will, Kenny." I say as I get into my car. He moves back and I drive away. What a good looking and smart guy! It's too bad someone can't fix him so he could function in society and live a better life. As I drive to the office, I think of how powerless we are over such illness. I realize how powerful the human mind, how magnificent and mysterious a machine it is. The mind is the most powerful thing on earth. If we could gain control over our own minds, we could control many things. But the complete workings of the human brain are still largely a mystery that God continues to keep from our reach.

The boss doesn't want to hear what I have to say about the incident with the IV. "Just do the work, get the hell out of there as quick as you can and turn in your billing on time!" Profit is his concern, not any concern I might try to discuss with him in our many brief meetings. "And for God sake can you just be pleasant to people and stop picking on the staff! It is not your concern if they don't get the tasks done. Let the home deal with them!"

"I know but I don't work for the home, Sir. I work for the patients and their needs come first." I say trying again to defend my position on getting care for the patients.

"Why do you have to take everything so fucking personally?" He rants. I know he is not expecting an answer as he continues yelling all rhetorical questions at me. "These patients aren't your fucking relatives!" I would like to tell him they are human beings with feelings and histories. Someone once loved then and someone may still love them. They lived and still live and were once contributing members of society. We should all care what happens to them as one day it may be one of us or one of our family members in a facility.

I say none of this because the man, I prefer to call Dr. Big Guy, with his cocky attitude, is not one to listen to an old woman. I'm at least twenty years his senior. He represents the new age of modern medicine. He is well dressed in a white linen shirt and gray dress pants. He is of slight build and has dark flawless skin. He's from the Middle East. I like his accent and the quirky way he uses the King's English. He has handed me a box of dates that he picked up in Dubai. I leave his office. I enter an exam room to see my first patient. I hope that whoever it is, hasn't over heard him rant at me like a deranged person. I should make more of an effort to bridge the gap in our differences on patient care but I just don't have the energy. He holds all the winning cards in this game. He is the Doctor, the one in charge. I am just the nurse practitioner, the subordinate who is supposed to always listen to the wise man, and follow his commands. Society dictates and we must defer to it. It's why my life has always been an uphill battle, against the wind; I constantly defy what it is that society dictates to women. "Be a good listener, be a good follower, defer, conform." As I approach retirement age, I find it harder to do than ever. Old age has not mellowed me in the least. In the back of my mind I can hear Bob Segar singing "Older now but still running against the wind."

Chapter 3

Later Night And On Call

After seeing another ten patients in the office, doing a ton of paper work, returning phone calls is the last thing I do before leaving. It's almost eight and dark outdoors. I have been going non-stop since eight in the morning. I drive to the Blue Whale, a quiet upscale sea food place. There are some drug sales representatives, doctors and other health care providers having a meeting for a briefing on a new medication. I slide quietly into my seat. The waiter comes to me right away and takes my order. I listen to the speaker as he touts the benefits of a new wonder drug for the elderly and infirmed. He makes it sound so good. Two of my friends, Nettie and Zev work for the drug company. They invite me to every one of their dinners. The food is good, what I can eat of it. I'm so tired that it's hard to keep my eyes open.

When the meeting is over Zev walks me to my car. He encircles me in his arms like I'm a small lost child. My friends and some of my family members think I've lost my mind for hanging out with a black man. We meet up once or twice a month to talk and have dinner and a few laughs. It seems to ease the pain of our everyday work lives. Zev is a tall, slender man who is well educated. He's very talented and knows how to be a friend. "It will get better after you retire, Mary, I just know it will". He says. I give him a knowing look because this man is seventy-five and shows no signs of retiring any time soon just as he shows little sign of aging. I feel I'm at least one hundred standing here with him.

"You're sure one to talk and give me advice on retirement". I say as I smile up at him. He gives me a squeeze. I know he still can't see himself as retired and staying home all day. He plays the best jazz sax I've ever heard. I go to clubs and listen to him whenever he has a gig around town. It's why he has such a good attitude toward everything. I think his music is his outlet. All these years, I would have done well to have such a diversion instead of dedicating every waking minute to health care and the rearing of my children. I might have become more tolerate if I had perfected my musical abilities. I think I buried my love of music because the weight of responsibility fell totally on me when my tall dark handsome musician husband left me for another woman. But that's all water under the old bridge now.

Zev and Nettie are two of the most talented people I know. It never ceases to amaze me that the greater population was so awestruck with President Obama. He isn't the only black man who ever put on a suit, speaks perfect English and has a Harvard Law degree. No offence to our wonderful president but I think this is such a put down to all people of color. My two friends are some of the best educated and wisest people I know. They help me to see the humor in my day. I tell them stories about the places I go and the stuff that happens there, leaving out the names and exact places to protect the innocent as well as the guilty. They roar with laughter and tell me I should write a book.

Home at last! I clean up, slip into bed and turn on Late Night TV for a little comic relief. The Jay Leno monologue is nearly over when the first call comes in. I'm on call every night for the five nursing homes I cover for the medical practice that employs me. I'm also on call for Leda, a fact I didn't learn until reaching the office this afternoon. She is out of town, again, for the week.

The first call is from Pleasantville. This is one of Leda's homes. It was mine until she came on board a few months ago. I had a lot of problems there so the boss took it away from me and give it to her.

From the way she talks about it, I gather not much has changed there since she took over. She calls it Death Ville because so many people die very soon after admission.

"Miss Mary dis da nurse on three south at Pleasantville. I got Mr. Briggs here and his testicles is swollen". She tells me and then gives me his vital signs. I mull all the information over in my head along with what I already know about Mr. Briggs. I order some lab work, an antibiotic and pain pills for the patient. I request that an ice bag be placed under the scrotum for comfort. "But Miss Mary" the nurse replies, "I tole ya his testicles is swole, he ain't got no scrotum."

"Excuse me?" I say as politely as I can "are you a nurse?" I ask. "Yeah! Of course I'm a nurse." She replies.

"Well then you must know that the scrotum is the sack that houses the testicles and an ice bag applied there will ease the pain and swelling." I tell her trying my best to explain the male anatomy. "Please do the orders as soon as possible? I'll come in the morning to see Mr. Briggs."

"Well I still don't know what you talkin bout but I call the supervisor and ask her to help." I thank her and hang up hoping the man will get some kind of relief.

The next call comes in about ten minutes later. It is Pleasantville again. "Miss Mary dis Lucy on one east how you?" she asks.

"I'm fine Lucy" I reply. "How are you?"

"Oh Izz good, Miss Mary but we sho do miss you round here." She tells me, I am truly touched. "Why thank you Lucy, I appreciate that" I say.

Lucy takes a deep breath and continues "Yah, well Miss Mary, I be readin dees here reports dat come in from the x-ray place and dis one on Mrs. Long say she got a dick in her back. I don't think no woman could got a dick!"

"Lucy could you read me just what it says under the heading of impression at the very end?" I ask.

She reads in her best voice "Degeneration dick disease of the lower spine. Now what do you think a that?"

I try to contain myself as I repeat back to her "Lucy it says degenerative disc d-i-s-c (I spell it out for her) disease of the lower spine."

I explain there is no dick in the woman's back. I ask her to place the report in my box so I can check it in the morning when I arrive.

The next call is from a different home. Thank God! I think to myself. But my relief soon fades away as the caller identifies herself and tells me "Miss Mary, yo patient has an orgasm in her urine report." I want to ask if she enjoyed it but I know that the joke would be lost on this one and I am very tired by now.

"What kind of ORGANISM IS IT?" I ask with great emphasis. She tries her best to tell me what it is called but she is unable to pronounce the word properly so she tries to spell it. I now know what type of infection it is. "Zoey read the list below that will tell us what type of medication will work on this ORGANISM in order to get rid of it, please?" One again she is unable to pronounce any of the words and she gets tongue tied trying to spell them to me. She also can't tell me if there is an R or an S after the medication which would indicate if it will kill the organism (I would like to say here I want one that won't kill the orgasm either but I don't.) Since she is unable to articulate, I am at a loss as to what to order for the patient. After twenty minutes of trying to get information out of her, I'm all out of patience with her and myself. I tell her to put the report in my box; I will see it in the morning and order something. I feel safe in doing so because the patient is not exhibiting any signs of illness or running a fever. I know some of these infections can be chronic.

After a few more calls and many minutes spent hashing over in my mind all the events of the day, I finally fall asleep. Suddenly its morning and I've only slept about two and a half hours. I've never been a good sleeper anyway and less so in my old age. I have functioned on less sleep in my life time. It's another beautiful day like the one before. But I realize that it has been made longer by these two extra visits to different homes I must make. I thank God anyway for this day. He has, after all, chosen to give me one more.

I try to look at each day as a gift from God. I admit that I didn't always. Since my first bout with cancer, I am aware that each day is another blessing. I try to make the best of it if I can. A cancer survivor can't be too thankful for another day. Although, on such a day as this one, I do wonder why I have survived and others have not been so fortunate. I've had breast cancer twice and have had both of my breasts removed. I try not to question God too much about why I survived it. I find trying to do the best you can is the only answer. We can never know or fully understand God's plan for us. I feel that I just have to work harder to deserve the time I have been given.

Chapter 4

Putting Out The Fire

The wavy lines of heat are coming off the black top paving of the parking lot at Pleasantville. It's another hot early fall day. The stench from the building is unbearable as I enter. Millie prints my list for me. "I'm so glad to see you here". She's one of the few nice human beings working here. She seems to enjoy her job as receptionist and switch board operator. She is an enormous woman with light brown curly hair. She wears glasses so thick they look like the bottom old glass coca cola bottles. She never seems to have a bad day. She is always pleasant and smiling. I silently thank God for simple honest caring people like her. They truly make the world go round.

"Thank you Millie" I reply. "It's nice to see you again, too."

I head up to Mr. Briggs, who, indeed, has a swollen scrotum the size of a basketball. I examine him first. He is in obvious pain and he continues to run a fever. "I'm going to send him to the hospital." I tell the floor nurse. As I walk down the hall to the nurse's station. The supervisor is hot on my heels right behind me.

"Why are you sending him out?!" she demands. "Whatever he needs we can do it here."

"I'm afraid he is in septic shock. He has altered mental status now and can no longer give me an answer to any question that makes sense." I tell her. Mr. Briggs has been a very good patient. He was quite alert and perfectly rational the whole time he has been in the home up. "He will need IV fluids and IV antibiotics as well as blood cultures and many other tests."

She gives me a look of utter scorn and walks away after I tell her, "All the orders I gave last night have not been done and won't be carried out for at least the next two days. It may be too late by then for this very nice elderly gentleman who has a son that cares very much about what happens to him." This reality has silenced her for the moment. She doesn't have a comeback for me. I know she will take this high in the chain of command here at Pleasantville.

All medications have to come from whatever pharmacy the home has a contract with to provide them. Orders are sent there via fax. The meds are then delivered by a carrier. It sometimes takes forty-eight hours or even longer for the medications to arrive.

"I can feel someone standing over me as I write the orders. I look up to see Ralph staring down at me. "Well Mary," he says. "I take it that you are doing your best to keep the patients here in house? I know you want to keep our census up." Ralph is the administrator of the home and the brother-in-law of the owner of this particular chain of nursing homes. Keeping the census up and maintaining a steady flow of revenue is his main job. "You know that's why we have you here don't you?" he has a full grin fixed on his face.

He gives me the creeps in his fine suit that I'm sure costs over a thousand dollars. He is eyeing me up and down. I know I should not respond to this kind of condescending talk from him but I can't help it. "I'm here to take good care of the patients, Sir, which is what I'm doing." He does not pay me. The doctor that owns the practice that employs me pays my salary. I know they're good friends, he and Dr. Big Guy. My pert replies will go directly there. "When a patient is critically ill, I must hospitalize him for treatment. A dead patent yields no revenue and also causes an empty bed." Oh! Why can't I just keep my mouth shut at times like these! I think to myself. The smirk never leaves his face as he walks away from me.

The nursing home does not get paid if a patient goes back into the hospital and they must hold his bed open for three days as well as relinquish the revenue to the hospital for the patient's care. The other real problem here is they want the revenue but want to spend little of it to care for the patient. The home does not have intake coordinators who look at the cost of taking care of the patient before they are accepted for admission. Some of the patients require lots of care and special medications. Some IV antibiotics can cost one thousand dollars per dose or more. The home has to bear the cost. So they take the patient and then want me to give the cheapest thing possible to the patient in place of the expensive one. It is almost never possible. Super bugs require super antibiotics and they cost money.

On the second floor the charge nurse catches me. Mimi is someone for whom I have little regard. She is a small youngish woman of Asian descent who has no respect for me or the patients in her care. She loves to order me about the place. I guess it makes her feel important and more authoritative in the eyes of the staff. "Dee-Dee in 201 needs her anti-seizure medication changed or you need to give her a bigger dose of it" she says as she shoves a lab report of the patient's drug level in front of my face. The level in Dee Dee's blood is very low. It is what we would call non-therapeutic. The resident she is referring to is well known to me. She has no family and is a ward of the state. The young female in her forties is non-verbal and non-responsive to everything but pain. She makes no eye contact. There is no sign that she hears or understands what is going on around her. Therefore, she is the easiest patient to ignore. She is fed through a tube in the upper abdomen. The feeding is on what is known as a pump.

"Well, are you going to do it?" she asks in a snide tone.

"Has she had any seizures?" I ask already knowing the answer is no. Mimi shakes her head.

"Ok, so please make sure the staff is following the protocol for administering these drugs via the feeding tube." I already know they don't follow it. If they did, Mimi and I wouldn't even be having this conversation. The patient is cleaned up in the morning and the tube feeding with all her meds for the entire day are crushed up and put into it. The meds will include every dose due her including her sleeping pill for the night. It's done so the nurse and the staff will not have to come back to attend her until the evening shift. After completing these tasks, the medication nurse can then go off the floor on a break, or have a smoke. She will feel very proud of herself for having finished passing all of the meds to the patients on time. The supervisors and administrators think she is wonderful and so efficient. For Dee-Dee, it means that she is not getting any of the meds at the proper times nor are they being administered to insure proper absorption. Hence, the patient's blood level of the drug is non-therapeutic.

I write an order for the tube feeding to be turned off for an hour before and after the seizure med is given and for the feeding tube to be flushed with at least one cup of water before and after giving any meds. It is a lot of work for the staff and they don't like it. I also write for the test to be repeated in two weeks but order no change in the mediation or the dose. Mimi is very angry and jerks the order from my hand as I hold it out to her.

As I'm entering what I call the gang banger wing, I'm approached by Mariumamma. She is a nurse from India. She embraces me and kisses me on both cheeks European style. "Oh Miss Mary I am so glad to see you! Come I show you wounds I am working on." She is obsessed with wounds. I like a good open wound, myself, but I like the whole patient too. She is only interested in the wounds of these gang bangers who are quadriplegics and paraplegics.

Dante has had both of his legs burned off past his hips by a rival gang. I have learned that these gangs have rituals of punishment for one another. They don't always shoot to kill. They like to leave a live rival with permanent damage. They feel it carries a more powerful message of revenge than just killing a rival. It sends a potent warning to stay away from another gang's territory. Dante has adapted to nursing home life and is doing quite well. As far as can be determined, he has curtailed his gang activities. His wounds are healing nicely and he buzzes around in his motorized wheelchair participating in social activities at the home. He seems happy here despite the grave injuries he has sustained at the hands of a rival gang. The state goes to great lengths to keep rival gangs out of the same nursing home. Crypts and Bloods are never in the same home with Latin Kings and Skye.

Some of the young men and women have been wounded by police in gun battles prior to winding up in the nursing home. Reimbursement for care of these patients is very high. So homes like to take them. However, they are sometimes very difficult to deal with because they are still involved in gang activities. Others have learned the error of their ways and are reformed. They go out into the community and give talks on gang violence. They try to help communities rid themselves of gangs. Most of them never seem to be short of money to spend on whatever they please. Some still make a good living dealing in illegal activities; therefore, lots of pizza, Jack Daniels and illicit drugs floating around the place.

The staff does not like to find such items, but when they do, they call on me to come and confiscate it. I can't legally go into a patients things and take anything but if it is in plain sight, illegal, detrimental to the patient and the health and safety of others in the home, I can bring it to the desk. The family is then called to come and get it. If he or she has no family then I call the state guardian in charge of the patient, if there is one, or the social worker on that floor and the two of us dispose of it. I can't tell you how many times I have walked around here toting bottles of Jack Daniels and Absolute Vodka. I have Mac James's bottle tucked under my arm right today. He is following me down the hall very drunk. He is yelling that he needs the booze to kill his pain because the nurse won't give him pain pills. I write an order for him to get a hefty dose of vicodin every four hours as needed for pain. I know Leda will be getting another bottle from him when she returns.

I can't just call the police and turn them in for illegal activities. I'm not an employee of the home and I have no real authority. The home also doesn't want the authorities involved because they don't want the patients taken away as this will cause loss of revenue. They also don't want any negative publicity. The home would not want to call attention to the fact that illicit drugs and alcohol are being used freely within the facility. Everyone here tries to treat the problem first even when a patient takes an over dose or gets dangerously intoxicated. When all options have been exhausted and no other solution is possible, then a private ambulance is called and the patient is taken to the nearest emergency room with the diagnosis of mental status changes. The administrators of the home will plead innocent to knowing anything about drugs or alcohol.

There are times when a patient, who is mentally unstable, will call the police and tell them that he or she is being held against their will. An officer is sent to investigate the matter and discovers that the patient is not lucid. These calls are a lot of paper work for the department. They are obligated, by law, to investigate every one of these calls. The home is then given a warning to prevent such incidents from occurring again.

When a patient or family member calls the state agency responsible for overseeing any wrong doing in a facility, it is a really big deal. The agency will send out a team to investigate without warning the institution that they are coming or why. An 8x10 pink sign is posted in the lobby and in each elevator stating the department of public health is in the building conducting an investigation. Quietly, without giving names, the investigation of the complaint alleged is conducted.

I had to give a deposition to the state when one of our patients filed a complaint against Pleasantville. Dr. Big Guy was very nervous and worried that I would say the wrong thing and cause the state to sanction the home or move to close it. He knows I will not lie or cover up any wrong doing. Since he is the medical director for Pleasantville, he doesn't want it to happen for many reasons. First of all, it is a loss of revenue for him and the publicity is very damaging.

The patient who filed the complaint, I knew well. The allegations she professed were unfounded and I had written documentation to prove it. Dina Jane was a paraplegic and because she is paralyzed from the waist down, she sits in a wheelchair all day. Most of the time she sat in her chair for more than twelve hours at a time. Therefore, she developed many large deep open wounds on her buttocks and hips. She never wants to lay long enough for her treatments to be effective so her wounds could heal. While in her automated chair, she had no control over bowel or bladder, therefore, she sat in her own excrement all day. She liked to spend time in the smoke room puffing away and flirting with the male patients that hung around there. As a result, her wounds became worse and also infected causing her to become gravely ill. She was sent to the hospital by me more than once in septic shock.

After her last admission, she filed a complaint against the home alleging the nurses were not caring for her wounds. I knew it to be untrue; I had documented the patient's behavior and refusal of treatment. I had all the nurses document as well, each time she refused the dressing changes. Pleasantville is a bad place and probably needs to be shut down. I just couldn't let it happen over a case that was unfounded. I brought all the documentation to the attention of the state investigator when I met with him. I was able to answer all his questions and show that the patient's claims were unfounded. "Good Job! The home and the state said you were wonderful, they were very impressed. How did you do it?" Dr. Big Guy wanted to know, as he slapped me on the back.

I merely looked at him and said, "I only told the truth and showed them the documentation of all the times the patient refused to lay in bed for the treatment of the wounds and the dressing changes." There was also evidence of her refusal to take her medications on time for the infected wounds.

"Amazing! That is just Amazing," he repeats again. I was dumbfounded. I could see nothing to be amazed about, it was only fact to me.

I have a few patients here on the gang banger wing; however, none of mine are model citizens. Mariumamma shows me some wounds that we call decubitus ulcers. They are big enough to stick your head through. Under her care I see that they are clean and with good new tissue formation in them. She consults with me about different treatment modalities. "You are the expert on all of the latest products so you tell me what you think works best and I will order it." I tell her.

Mariumamma is worth her weight in gold but I notice that she is oblivious to the pain that these patients are in when she is working with their wounds. She tends to toss them all around like rag dolls. As she is tossing them around and showing me the treatments and the progress she has made, I try to give comfort and acknowledgement to the patients. I run behind her and give some pain medications to each individual patient. I get caught up in the pain and suffering of these people while Mariumamma is reveling in her work on their wounds.

But I think together we're a good team. When we are done we have made some progress. It isn't enough to satisfy my need for a better outcome for my patients but it is significant.

Smoking among the gang bangers on this wing is a real problem but the home refuses to address it or acknowledge it exists. They smoke in their beds, which is against the law. They have no way of controlling or disciplining the offenders. They also don't want to for fear of loss of revenue. The staff has to throw out a lot of burnt mattresses into the dumpster out in back of the home. They do this in the dark of night and make sure that they are under all the garbage so they will be compressed into it and never seen by anyone. Garbage is picked up by a private scavenger company and not by the city in which the home is located. No fire alarm is ever called. No lectures on the dangers of smoking in bed are ever given. There is no strict no smoking policy ever enforced.

Sheila the social worker joins us on our rounds. She excuses herself as we examine wounds and then comes back for her part of the visit with each patient. She really puts her whole heart and soul into the care she gives the residents on this wing. Sheila is as tall lying down as she is standing up. She dresses quite well for a single mom in her forties. The thing that gets to me about her is this: no matter how nasty people get with her she never loses her cool and calm demeanor. The expression on her very large round well made-up face always remains pleasant. She and Mariumamma are the bright shining stars of this institution. Without them, I think the state would have closed the doors here long ago. I wonder for a few seconds if Ralph is aware of this fact or if he even cares.

The lunch hour draws near and I take Sheila and Mariumamma for a good meal at Murphy's. It is just across the highway from the home. The restaurant has good food that is served hot and quick in a comfortable environment. I like to reward the staff members that work so hard for the people in their care. I watch them smile as they enjoy the meal. I know for them there are few rewards or accolades, no commendations or major awards. They won't even receive "a leg lamp" for their many heroic efforts on behalf of the patients they serve. It hurts my heart to think of how many of these wonderful people I have known in my years of practice. They work until they die in the service of others. Most of these places do not know or appreciate them for what they are and what they have done for the institutions they serve. To me they are the most selfless humans I have ever had the pleasure of knowing. They go on day in and day out and never seem to be fazed by the bad lot they have been given. They perform back breaking work for little pay with no recognition from patients or from those who employ them. I hope God sees them and can make a better place for them in the hereafter. These tiny spokes in the big wheel of life are what makes the world go round. The world does not turn because of the loud boasting people who blow their own horn about how great they are and all they have done in the service of mankind.

Chapter 5

Beautiful People With Beautiful Souls

I have spent the whole day at Pleasantville and I've seen about twenty-two patients. I have read many reports and written many orders. My fingers ache and my feet are sore. A dull headache pounds at my temples as a feeling of exhaustion threatens to overtake me when I leave the building. Suddenly Mariumamma appears out of nowhere "You come with me". She says with some authority. I follow her too tired to protest. We get into her car and she drives to a part of the city I have never seen before. She stops the car in front of a little shop. When we get out I notice that she is no longer wearing her white uniform. She has on a brightly colored sari made of beautiful material in orange with gold threads in a flower pattern all over it. She is wearing turquoise jewelry set in gold. I can't guess what the sari is made of but it is dazzling. The heavy necklace and earrings of large blue stones set it off perfectly.

The street is crowded and people are calling to her with joyful greetings "Mamasan! Mamasan!" they shout. Some are holding up beautifully made garments and jewels while others hold out food. I see now that there are many shops and shop keepers all over the street. We come closer and they all speak to Mariumamma is a language that I don't understand. They bow their heads in a friendly greeting. Her arms are becoming full of many exquisite things as we pass by all the shops but I see little money changing hands.

"How can they afford to let these things go for so little?" I ask as we are lead to a table and seated at an outside café.

"I take care of them and they take care of me," the Mamasan replies in a quiet voice with down cast eyes. "These things they are for you anyway" she sees the puzzled look on my face and she goes on. "Really Miss Mary, people here know how good you are to me and the ones in your care. Please don't disappoint them by not accepting their gifts and my gifts to you." I want to let loose and cry as my eyes fill with tears. This experience is both elation and a humbling all at the same time. I feel overwhelmed with emotion and can hardly speak.

We are not allowed, as professional nurses, to accept any gift of money or other things. I try never to do it. But this is a strange situation that I cannot get out of easily without causing offence. Knowing this, I am still too overwhelmed to speak. Tears come to my eyes as she orders food for both of us. "We eat now," she says as a wonderful meal of Indian food is served to us hot and spicy. I have no clue what it is but it tastes marvelous as I eat hungrily. I can see she is pleased that I enjoy the food.

I'm trying not to cry as Mariumamma and I part company. I am loaded down with all kinds of beautiful things for my granddaughters and even several hand caved toy swords for my grandsons. They will be so excited with this stuff. I check my watch when I'm back in my car and note that it is ten o'clock already. There is no reason to go back to the office. The service has been locating me without difficulty and I have received a page about every fifteen minutes since we left the nursing home. I pray for at least five hours of sleep tonight as I head for home.

Home in my bed I wish that I could be more like Mariumamma and Sheila. I wish I could ignore the things that go on around me and just focus on doing the best job I can. I don't know why the poor conditions of these homes grate on my every nerve. They cause me to feel helpless and defeated as if nothing I do makes any difference at all. This kind of thinking does nothing but make me to toss and turn for the better part of the night. Not even the Jay Leno monologue can make me laugh or raise me out of my depressed state. It is never easy for me to put things out of my mind and let sleep overtake me.

When I finally drift off, I dream of a house with many rooms, all different, one opening up to another. As I walk from one to another, a sense of peace comes over me. I drift farther into sleep wondering where I am and who lives in this magnificent home. I turn and I am aware of a great light. Then my eyes fly open and I realize I was dreaming as morning light pours into my large master bedroom. I have slept well for at least five glorious hours.

Remembering that dream as I shower and dress for the day, whose house was it where I walked? This sweet remembrance brings to mind a passage from the Good Book of the News of Christ our Lord who said "In my Father's house there are many rooms." It is with renewed courage and conviction that I begin my day once again. I acknowledge that I have been given yet another day. Thank you, dear God for it does not matter what it may bring.

Chapter 6

Life Is What You Make It, Really?

Once I'm in my car, I try to ready myself to go back to nursing and rehab center number one. I may have forgotten to mention the name of this facility, it is called Sunny Place and it is anything but sunny! The home is considered one of the best in the area. It is quite expensive to stay there. Maybe this is how it got its name because Sunny money pit could best describe it, I think.

Kitty Wells is singing "It wasn't God who made Honky Tonk Angels". The tune has followed Tennessee Ernie Ford who sang "sixteen tons and what do you get, another day older and deeper in debit. Saint Peter don't you call me cause I can't go, I owe my soul to the company store…." The music is calling this ex honky tonk angel to work. The story of my past life will have to wait for another time. I can't let my mind drift to the past. There is too much work to do in my near future.

My family can't understand why I have to listen to this early forties and fifties country music. This is the type I grew up hearing down on the farm. The music playing on the radio was my only connection with the outside world. I would listen for hours while my mother tended the animals, hoed in the garden, and did the wash in an old iron tub we had in our basement. Tennessee Ernie, Hank

Williams, Hank Snow, Red Foley, Ernest Tub, and Pasty Montana were the friends I played with all day. I still know all the words to these old tunes all these sixty some years later.

When my oldest sister came home from school she immediately changed the station to her stories of the afternoon. We would listen to "Portia Faces Life" then "Young Dr. Malone" and "Stella Dallas". They were her favorite ones. When the boys came in and my father came home from work then it was "The Lone Ranger" and "Gene Autry" until bed time. Since my parents didn't send me to school as they did my siblings, the radio was my world. The county said I wasn't ready and I never knew why. I didn't start going until I was almost eight years old.

People back then didn't have TV yet. Oh I'm not saying that it wasn't invented yet, I'm not that old! Well almost. Most people of middle or lower income in my farm community could not afford a TV. We used to go to the neighbors and watch theirs on rare occasions. My father would take them his homemade wine and things from his garden. The TV screen was very small and we all sat on the floor around it. I never was able to stay awake for a whole program. I would wake the next morning at home in bed and not recall how I got there.

My nose tells me I'm at my first destination of the day. I stop my musing of the past and go into the building. I see Johanna coming toward me. She is glowing all over in that bright morning sun streaming through the big windows. She is a young girl with a beautiful soul. You can see it in her green eyes that are so expressive. She is most likely about twenty-eight years old. I know this is her first job as a Nurse Practitioner. The center hired her to see patients who have become ill. She then calls the physician after she makes a complete assessment and advises him of the patient's condition. She relies on me a lot to help her make clinical decisions because she is not totally sure of her own judgment yet. She tries to do a good job here with little or no support from the staff or administration. The main goal in all of these nursing homes is to keep the patients in them as long as possible, as long as they meet the criteria for admission and care. Once they can no longer justify the stay or the insurance has run out, they get rid of the patient as soon as possible. They may be sent to another lower level of care home, group home or home with relatives if they have any willing to take them in.

The bright sun is spilling all over Johanna's red hair as she comes closer. "I don't understand this lab report." She says as she hands it to me. I can see it is a urinalysis result on a patient that I don't have on my list.

"It looks normal enough to me." I reply.

"Yes but look what it says on the bottom of the page." My eyes go to the last sentence and I read "Multiple sperm noted in specimen," the report is on a female according to the name above.

"Oh," I say trying to be casual about it. "How old is this patient and does she have a husband or significant other that visits her regularly?" I ask hoping that this will solve the mystery.

Johanna looks distress and she says, "She is a new patient here she is non-verbal and non-responsive. Her visitors do not include any males." I feel by breakfast coming up in my throat. I swallow hard and try to maintain my composure. I see by the date of birth on the report that she is about seventy-five years old.

"Johanna if there is no male who visits her then you should report this to administration as soon as possible." I tell her. I hate to hear this kind of stuff! It brings me down for the rest of the day. I can't eat at all when I meet with Zev and Nettie for a drug company sponsored dinner later that night. I can't concentrate on what is going on. All I can think about is that poor woman and my mind runs wild thinking of what might have happened to her.

Zev leans and whispers in my ear, "The light at the end of the retirement tunnel is shining brighter." He is always saying such things to me to try and cheer me up when I am feeling down. But I can't see any bright light tonight. I can't even tell him why I'm so distraught. I can't talk about a case like this for fear it will have bad repercussions so I say nothing. I know that Zev takes care of his Ninety-eight year old mother. Although Ulla May is quite spry he has to leave her with a care giver while he is at work. It would upset him to hear of a case of possible abuse.

I feel awful that night and all the next day. I feel anger and powerlessness so strong that my knees are shaking when I stand. "What in the hell is wrong with you today? You look like shit!" yells Dr. Big Guy. I can't tell him what has transpired with another Doctor's patient. I'm sure he wouldn't believe me if I told him. He loves these nursing homes and they love him. He turns a blind eye to all their imperfections. He defends their lack of trained staff and sides with them in any dispute that may arise. He will side with the home every time even if it is me or a family or even the state bringing up issues. Dr. Big Guy's position at a lot of the homes is that of Medical Director. He gets paid a lot of money to do this work. But as I see it, it isn't much of a job. He only has to show up at a staff meeting once a month or so and as long as he sees the patients once every sixty days he meets all state requirements for their care. Nurse practitioners like me, Leda and Johanna do all the work. We call him if we need help or can't decide on a plan of care for an individual patient. I try not to call him because his answers are not always what I want to hear. I'm older than he is and I have been doing this work for much longer. We have a collaborative relationship and not one of direct supervision. Nurse practitioners are responsible for their own actions in this state.

Once I received a call from one of the other rehab centers from a nurse who wanted to know where she should send Mrs. Jones for a feeding tube placement. "Is it a gastric feeding tube placement?" I asked. "Why I don't really think she needs one because if you feed her she will eat everything on her tray." I know this because when I was there making rounds I fed her dinner myself and she ate it all.

"Well I have an order here from the doctor to send her out for a feeding tube." She tells me.

"Ok, I'll go ask Doctor and I will call you back, thank you." I reply and hang up. I find the good Dr. Big Guy sitting in his office. His feet are up on his desk and he is leaning back in his big chair talking to someone on the phone. It is a woman and I sure it is not Mrs. Big Guy by the sound of the conversation. I exit quickly and wait until he is done and calls me in.

"What is it Mary?" he asks sounding rather irritated.

"I just need to know if you really want a feeding tube inserted into Mrs. Jones. I found that she will eat very well if she is feed." I say with confidence.

"What in the living hell are you talking about?" he yells at the top of his lungs so the whole office can hear him. "Nurses do not have time to feed every patient who won't eat! Just get the fucking tubes put in and have done with it!" I am mortified but reframe from saying anything. I remind myself that I have lots of responsibility but little authority. My saying or doing anything other than what he tells me to do, once I have consulted his opinion, could result in dismissal even though I know in my heart that this is barbaric treatment of the elderly. I know it is done everywhere and I want to cry because we seem to punish those who have lost the ability to help themselves. We solve their problems by the most convenient way for us. I call a GI specialist and tell him I will put the patient in the hospital for a period of twenty-three hours for the procedure. He agrees and thanking me for doing all the paperwork.

A few days later when I arrive back at Sunny Place Rehab Center I intend to find Johanna and ask her about the patient with the sperm in her urine. My rounds are pretty slow today for some reason. I enter my patient Alice's room. She happens to share it with the screamer, Arlene. She is the pretty woman with the wedding picture attacked to her wheelchair. I look over at Arlene's bed because she is so quiet. There is a pillow over her head. I run over and remove it. "Arlene, you ok!" she doesn't respond because she doesn't communicate with the exception of her screaming. Her skin is warm and dry and she is breathing at a normal rate. "Alice do you know what is wrong with Arlene?" She shakes her head and I run into the hall to ask the nurse to check on her. The nurse waves her hand to indicate she will get to it later. I can do no more since she is not my patient.

The rounds for Sunny Place are coming to an end when I find Johanna on another ward. I ask her about the urine as casually as I can since it is not any of my business. She smiles and looks very relieved. "I took it to the director of nursing and she told me that she called the lab and discovered that a mistake had been made. She told me I didn't have to worry about it anymore she took care of everything." I can see the relief in Johanna's face and I know that she wants to feel safe here so she believes what she has been told by the administration. But I know that there are many procedures in place in order to prevent any mistake in the handling of specimens and the likely hood of such an error is slim to none.

It's one of those times that I wish I wasn't so old. I still could be living in a time when I would have believed that administrator also. But I have seen too much over the years for that to be my reality. I walk through the halls and wonder about some of the male staff I see. Could it have been one of them? Sperm is easily detected and there could not have been a mistake unless it was another female's specimen. If there had been any discrepancy in the tracking numbers the machine which processes the specimen would have caught it.

When I visit my patient Alice who shares the room with the screamer over the next few weeks I find Arlene in that same odd position with the pillow over her face. I remove it each time and ask the nurse to check on her. I can't explain the strange finding and I can't really do anything about it as she is not my patient. I can do no more than I have already done.

It is Monday morning, a new day and a new week. I want it to be good and I don't want any more conflict between me and Dr. Big Guy. We have had some really big disagreements lately over the new computer system. "You are just too old for this new modern age of health care. You need to get with it and adapt to it and be more flexible." He tells me.

"It isn't the computer but the program itself, sir, which is the problem. It doesn't meet the needs of our practice." I reply trying to explain what it is about the system that makes it difficult to use.

"You don't even know what the hell you are talking about!" he grumbles and walks out on our conversation. I shouldn't paint him too harshly as he does try to be fair with me now and then. One night, he came to me as I was preparing to leave the office quite late. He noticed the time and that I was still there. "You know I do appreciate how hard you work even if I do not understand why you get so emotional about a bunch of old people who are going to die soon anyway." I wanted to reply that I don't understand why he cares so little when it is they that pay our bills and allow us to drive nice cars. We can send our kids to college and do all the things that were not possible for them in their day. But I say nothing as he leaves. Why I always feel so defeated when I talk to him I just don't know.

A few minutes later, he comes back in. "Look would you like to go with me to a wine tasting party at the country club tonight? It is my way of rewarding you for a job well done." He says with a sincere look on his face. I can read between the lines because he knows I don't drink ever! I hate the smell of booze. I also know that he is meeting all those young girls that he likes. He has several of them employed here in the office. His wife won't be upset if he tells her that he took me out to dinner as a reward. She knows that I'm more than twenty years his senior and as old as his mother. Even if he is just using me as his alibi I feel honored that he asked. I feel he wants me to know he acknowledges my work. I decline his invitation saying that I don't drink ever. He smiles and says that he understands which I'm sure he does not. I thank him again as he heads for the door.

Thinking back to my young years, I know this was not the way it was then. My father made wine when I was a little girl. I loved the smell of the fermenting grapes in the wine cellar. I would go in there and lay down under one of the big wooden barrels and turn the wood spout to a nice steady drip, drip, drip. I would drink all the wine I wanted. In later years, however, I could not tolerate the smell or taste of any type of alcoholic beverage. In my years as a young adult, I did my share of drinking alcohol but I suddenly developed intolerance for it. Sometime in my thirties it gave me a throbbing pain in the vessel of my neck. I knew this to be a bad sign of things to come and choose to ignore it. I didn't drink beverage of this type again.

Sunny Place comes into my view and I pull into it while Marty Robbins is singing "Well I never felt more like singin the blues cause I never thought that I'd ever lose your love dear…..you got me singin the blues." The song fits the day. It is gray out and a soft rain is falling. The air is heavy with humidity and it is still warm although it is late fall. Sunny Place seems anything but sunny to me today.

Alice is up in her wheelchair waiting to go to therapy when I walk in. She has a sad look on her face. I look over at the screamer's bed and it is totally vacant. "Alice where is Arlene? What happened to her did she go to the hospital?" She shakes her head and just stares out the window. I can't ask any more questions of anyone or I will be in violation of the HIPPA laws. These laws were drafted during the Clinton Administration and put into law after President Bush took office. Basically it states that no one can access information about a patient without the direct consent of said patient or his or her power of attorney. The Health Insurance Privacy and Portability Act kept information about patients I was not directly responsible for off limits to me.

Yes life is what you make it but do we really have any control over our own destiny? Marty Robbins is right I never felt more like singing the blues myself. I can't find out what happened to Arlene and I most likely never will. I hate to think that she met with foul play but it looks mighty suspicious. I can't go to Dr. Big Guy either. He would just think I'm crazy and maybe I am. Arlene could have just died of natural causes from one of the many diseases of old age. The haunting sight of her with that pillow over her face every time I saw her these last few weeks will not leave me. What can I do? Call the state in to investigate? Report it to the police? None of these are options I can take. I have to work and I have no real concrete evidence of any wrong doing. I guess life is what you make of it as long as you have all your faculties and can control some portion of it. For those who are not so fortunate, well it is up to the rest of us to help them if we can but sometimes we just can't. My spirits are spiraling down into some kind of depression but I just can't help myself. I swing the big town car onto the highway and I head for home, defeated once again.

Chapter 7

The Light At The End Of The Retirement Tunnel

A warm happy feeling comes over me; I'm excited making this trip to the social security office. It is a hot summer day. I have been planning this for a very long time. I'm going to find out what my income will be if I retire this year. I have an appointment but I still end up waiting for over an hour before I am called. A pleasant woman in a cubical asks if she can help me. I'm a little mad now that I had to wait so long before being called. "Well it is just the way it is around here we never know how long an individual appointment will take ma'am. Please raise you right hand and swear to tell the truth the whole truth and nothing but…." I can't believe I have to do this as I promise to tell the truth about all of my income over the last forty-six years!

She has records on every penny I ever made in my entire life so the swearing thing is totally baffling to me. She gives me the low down on all I need to know in order to retire by my next birthday. She shows me that working longer will actually cost me some income. It is spring now and my birthday is in the fall. I have started counting the days marking them off on my calendar one by one. It surprises me to learn I will have to pay for Medicare even though I have been doing so since it became law in 1965!

The money I will receive from social security and my pension will still not afford me the lifestyle I have become accustomed. I will have to work at least one or two days a week to supplement it. I will not be working for Dr. Big Guy but another physician whom I have known for many years. Dr. Nelson, Dr. Mild Mannered, as I will refer to him, is really alright. I have worked with him for many years one day a week. He is quiet and very conservative. We understand each other and he pretty much leaves me alone when it comes to my work. I don't bug him all the time either. I work out of his office about eight hours a week now so I am looking forward to a real life after retirement. There will be no more nursing homes to go to after I retire. This thought makes me both sad and happy at the same time. I love the elderly and will miss them but I hate the nursing homes and the sloppy care they give seems almost criminal. It's hard for me to believe I have turned into one of the old people I have cared for all of my life.

Now I am confronted with the task of having to tell Dr. Big Guy I will be retiring on my next birthday.

My friends have lots of advice for me on the subject of telling Dr. Big. Don't do it too soon most warn me. He could fire me, they tell me. Most people think that this is illegal. In some states it might be but in this state that is considered an "At Will" state, your boss can fire you for no reason if he or she chooses to do so. Discrimination suits are hard to bring about and cost a lot of money. My own attorney would love to sue Dr. Big Guy for many of the incidents of crude behavior and mistreatment I have endured over the last few years. My own lawyer thinks I am a push over as he has told me many times. The truth is that legal disputes stress me out more than just putting up with a bad situation. I believe that most people are like me otherwise there would be billions and trillions of law suits.

My lawyer feels that I'm too easy on the boss because of what happened last winter. I have never been sued and I can't see myself doing that to anyone else. People are sometimes oblivious to the pain and suffering that they inflict on others. Last winter I found myself alone in the office on a cold January night. I wasn't feeling well because I had suffered a bad nose bleed earlier that evening. All the young girls that work there keep the heat on eighty-five degrees all the time and it dries the air. I had a lot to do so I stayed late. When I was leaving the building there was no one else there. The parking lot was totally empty. I slipped and fell while coming out of the building because I didn't realize that snow had fallen that evening. The sidewalk in front of the one story building was covered with ice. I locked the door, turned around and my feet went out from under me! I landed on my right elbow and shoulder hitting it very hard. I slid down the cement ramp that leads up to the door. The ramp is a convenience so those in wheelchairs have easy access. It took me completely by surprise. My brief case went flying and so did my cell phone. I'm a heavy woman and I could not get myself up off the ground. My arm was hanging and I had no control over it. The pain was unbearable. I could only get to my knees and every time I tried to get up my arm would move and cause pain, nausea and dizziness. I crawled around looking for my cell phone. When I found it I dialed 911. No one answered and I tried one more time with still no answer. I tried to crawl up the icy ramp but I kept slipping backward. I was getting so cold I was shivering as it was only about twenty degrees outdoors. I was shaking badly. I was sure that my arm was broken, it was so painful. Hypothermia began to set in. My cell phone started to ring as I made another attempt to crawl up the cement ramp. I thought it was the service looking for me so I almost didn't answer it. "Did you call 911?" a voice said as I put the phone to my ear.

"Yes who are you!" I yelled into the phone.

"Well you don't have to yell. This is the dispatcher for the police department why are you calling 911?" She asked I couldn't believe this incredibly stupid question.

I took a deep breath and said "I'm calling because I've fallen outside my office building and I can't get up, my arm is broken!" I said breathlessly and quickly gave her the address of the building.

"I don't know where that is. Say it again." She commanded.

I can't believe this! The woman is the dispatcher for the city how could she not know this address! I repeat it again very exasperated by now and very cold. "Well the ambulance is right there, they should find you in less than two minutes." She replied. I looked up and saw the red lights flash and heard the siren. They pulled into the lot and two men got out toting a stretcher. They swiftly came across the lot to where I was on my knees on the ice.

"Don't try to pull me up!" I warned them. "I think both my right arm and shoulder are broken."

"Oh my God it's you Dr. Mary!" one of the paramedics cried out. Everyone in this region knows who I am if they are at all connected with the medical field. So, anonymity for me is not possible. I have cared for hundreds in the area and their family members. I may have worked with them somewhere in my long career. I hated that they call me Dr. Mary but I was too cold and in too much pain to correct them. I didn't care to address this wrong title bestowed upon me at that particular moment.

"Please just come here and steady my left side and I think I can stand." I said as calmly as I could for a woman with a broken bone. It worked fine and they got me off the ground quickly and onto the stretcher. In the ambulance they got to work on me right away.

"You sure did break your arm but I don't know about the shoulder. I just wouldn't move it if I were you," replied this young blonde man with an earnest face. After completing his assessment the paramedic let me make two phone calls. The first was to my answering service and the second was to my daughter.

"Sally, please get hold of Dr. Seal and let her know what has happened to me." I said. I knew that Dr. Big Guy had left town earlier that afternoon. He wasn't expected back for at least a week or more. I called my daughter and tried, in the calmest voice I could muster, to tell her what had happened. I told her was in good hands and on my way to the hospital.

"I locked up your car and it will be safe here we will keep an eye on It." said a police officer as he stuck his head in the back of the ambulance and handed over my keys and my purse. I always kept my purse locked in the car. I didn't even know that he was there or how he had gotten my car keys and my purse but I was in no condition to ask at the moment. I felt very fortunate the city contracted their ambulance service out to a private company with whom I was familiar.

Dr. Big Guy had left town earlier that day and the other physician in our practice was covering for him. I had asked the service to call her and let her know what had happened. My cell phone rang and when I answered she yelled into the phone. "Mary what happened the service told me you were injured! When you get to the hospital and they admit you tell them to put you under my name and I'll come there and take care of you."

"I'm sorry Doctor but you can't do that. You see we have an HMO plan and only the HMO doctor can take care of me. The reason I'm calling is that I'm afraid you will have to take my calls for a while." I said. It occurred to me how uninformed doctors are when it comes to insurance policies. They actually know less than the patients about how the insurance system works. I know, firsthand, the average patient knows absolutely nothing about how a policy works. She was not happy to hear that she would be doing triple duty now with me out of commission for God only knows how long.

When we reached the emergency room at the hospital somehow my daughter had already arrived. She was very upset to see me in such a state with my arm hanging in the paramedical splint. It looked like a piece of limp string cheese when the triage nurse removed the splint to examine the arm.

The x-rays showed that I had indeed fractured my right elbow and also totally dislocated it. This was determined after many hours of being in the emergence room. The doctor on duty tried several times to put it back in place. Some of these attempts were quit painful. He decided to give me some light anesthesia for the last attempt. I was still giddy and dizzy from this when he came into my room and said "Well kiddo, you really messed up this arm! I can't do anything with it. You will have to see an orthopedic surgeon at the HMO clinic in the morning."

I was to be sent home with my daughter. Before I could be released I needed to answer a bunch of questions and complete an enormous amount of paper work. I knew that I was a tad loopy from the anesthesia that I had been given. When they sent in a young new nurse to get my history and fill out the forms, I almost lost it completely. She was from the women's health unit. She had been sent down to the emergency room because they were so busy. As I looked around there were stretchers everywhere and the hallways were crowded with people. "Mrs. Michael, tell me when was your last menstrual period?" she asked in her most professional voice.

"I haven't had one in quite some time like twenty years maybe." I replied.

She blinked several times and stared at me saying "could you be pregnant!" I began to laugh hysterically! I could not stop while everyone stood by looking at me including my poor daughter. She was mortified but had the good sense to take over and finish the paper work.

My lovely calm and very mature daughter responded, "My mother has two grown daughters and we are in our forties. She has five grandchildren. May I answer any other questions you have in connection with her health status?" What a mature lovely and charming daughter I have, I thought to myself. I still cannot stop giggling over that last question.

The pretty young nurse, undeterred by my rude and unnatural behavior looked up with concerned eyes and said, "OK, but is your mother sexually active and could she be pregnant since she hasn't had a period in such a long time?" I then went into full blown hysterics with tears running down my face, I was laughing so hard. I began to fear that they would come in and give me more anesthetic or a psychiatric evaluation. I just couldn't stop laughing!

My daughter is one of those beautifully controlled individuals who can answer the most stupid question with respect and dignity. I saw the color drain from her face then replaced by a bright red hue. She continued her responses in the same manner with no help from me as I appeared to be headed for a complete mental breakdown.

When the paper work was completed, I was offered a prescription for a strong pain killer called vicodin. I turned it down as I was already three sheets to the wind, so to speak. I don't do well with this type of medication. "But everyone with such an injury as yours will need this form of stronger pain control." She replies. My daughter graciously accepted the prescription and thanked her for her help. I snorted again with giggles and laughter I can't seem to stop. Since

I couldn't get my pull over sweater back on, I had to go home in a hospital gown with my coat draped over my shoulders. I had to be wheeled out into the car port in order to get into my daughter's car so she could drive me home.

My lovely child tried to take me home with her but I refused. "I want to sleep in my own bed! It's almost three in the morning, I'm exhausted and so are you." Even though she was worried about my present mental state she gave in and took me home. Once she settled me into my bed she left with the promise to return first thing in the morning and drive me to the clinic. I had a fitful sleep and woke still wearing the hospital gown. I devised a way to take a shower by placing a large kitchen garbage bag over my affected arm and securing it with rubber bands to keep it in place and keep the arm from getting wet. It worked beautifully. I also proceeded to figure out how to dress myself. I was mortified by the way I looked. I really didn't relish leaving my home in such a state.

With my arm in a half cast, in that sling, I was unable to really dress myself properly. I put on the biggest thing I can find, a loose fitting fleece top. I couldn't get my breast prostheses and bra on with only one arm working. When my daughter arrived to take me to the HMO clinic she was quite surprised to see that I was able to do as well as I did. I struggled into my heavy coat as it was still very cold outdoors."Please try and control yourself today Mom, you embarrassed me so much at the hospital last night. I was so ashamed of your behavior." This caused me to have another laughing spell that I had a hard time stopping. I thought I had slept off the anesthesia from the emergency room but maybe not all of it.

Dr. Jones was a very stern looking orthopedic surgeon. He spent at least twenty minutes looking at my x-rays. He then made the most fantastic statement I had ever heard from a doctor in a long time. "I don't know what you expect me to do about this elbow. This thing is so messed up that no matter what I do you are not going to be able to have much use of your right arm."

I was shocked! "Excuse me, but I thought you were the orthopedic surgeon." I replied as my daughter standing next to me took in a deep breath.

"I am, but I can't perform miracles! I don't think you will get much use out of this arm again. I have to be honest with you" He replied.

"Bet me!" I yelled. "I have to work, use both of my arms just the same as you use both of yours!" "Mother please stop, be patient and cooperative." My daughter said, as always the dignified lady.

Dr. Jones then removed the ACE wrap and half splint/cast from my right arm. Thank God I am left handed. "Just brace yourself Mrs. Michael." He said, as he took my arm firmly and pulled it quickly high up popping my elbow back in place. The pain made me gasp! I was more than a little dizzy. I didn't want to yell and frighten others who might be waiting to see Dr. Jones. In a low steady voice, I let out every polite swear word that came to my mind.

"Holy Mother, God Almighty! For the love of ST. Peter! Fickle mother pickles!" I exclaim. My daughter turned very pale and stood crouching in the corner of the room. I then became aware that she might faint and hit the floor giving Dr. Jones two patients to look after. As my daughter recoiled Dr. Jones preceded to place a long white cast on my arm from finger tips to my shoulder with my whole arm in an upright position so that it looked as if I was waving at everyone. The pain subsided somewhat and I said to him, "Thanks Doc for fixing me." He took more x-rays at which he continued to stare for many minutes, causing my patience to dissipate. My daughter started shifting from foot to foot as she stood by me waiting for him to give instructions.

"Well you are not fixed. The elbow is back in place but the tip of the bone is completely broken off and I don't think I can do anything about it. It is sort of completely shattered. Please come back and see me on Monday." He replied. After surviving cancer twice, I have always been one to ignore pain and discouraging words from doctors. I would not have been standing there that day if I had, in the past, listened to this kind of talk and taken it seriously.

I got back into my coat and we start to walk across the lobby to exit the clinic. With my coat on and my arm up in the air like this it looked as if I was waving to all who passed by us. No one can see the cast so I just smiled at every one and nodded mouthing "Hello", once again, embarrassing my daughter.

"I'm getting the car." She blurted out and quickly exited the building leaving me standing in the lobby doing the queen's wave at everyone. In the car, I realized that I was going to have to let her take me home with her as I could do nothing with my right arm in this peculiar position.

The grandchildren were thrilled to hear I would be staying with them. They were jumping up and down and examining the large cast. My son-in-law, I could tell, was not thrilled or jumping up and down. He likes me well enough but I tend to make him nervous. Before I could get in the door and sit down the phone rang. It was Dr. Jones. He said that he wanted me to see his partner Dr. Walker for a second opinion. He had made all the arrangements for the appointment. I agreed to this plan and hung up the phone, resigning myself to a stay at the home of my younger daughter and her nervous husband.

The next several days went by slowly. I found myself falling asleep at the drop of a hat. I even dozed off in the middle of playing Barbie's with my granddaughter. I heard little Abby complaining to her mom that grandma had fallen asleep with Ken in her lap. I didn't realize until then, I was sleep deprived. I was always on call for my nursing homes. Without the constant phone calls, I began to see that I had been suffering from exhaustion as well as the affects from the anesthesia I had received in the emergency room. I found myself sleeping on and off no matter what was going on around me. Although I knew that I really needed the rest, I was bored to tears. I couldn't stop thinking about my patients at the nursing homes. My office patients I knew would be rescheduled and refills for their meds would be taken care of while I was away. The other reason I might have been so sleepy was that my daughter's house was just too warm for me. I keep the temp in my condo at sixty-five degrees all winter long, no matter what the temperature out of doors.

My daughter and her family are lovely people. I love them dearly but we are so different from one another. All of my friends, coworkers and others who have met my children always comment on what wonderful people they are. All tell me that they think I did something right in my life by raising two such lovely human beings. They are unlike their mother who is loud and opinionated about everything. I can see why others find it hard to believe that I am their mother.

Old age brings with it an altered pattern of sleep. I don't sleep for more than a few hours at a time. I get up frequently during the night. I sometimes need to use the bathroom. I was sleeping in the master bedroom so that I could have the TV on all night which has always been my habit. At two in the morning, I attempted to make a visit to the bath that is not connected to the master. I had to walk down a short hallway. I didn't want to turn on any lights for fear I might disturb someone. As I was quietly making my way there the door to the bedroom across the hall flew open. My son-in-law came running out "What's wrong are you sick? Do you need help!" before I could answer him he started calling for my daughter who appeared almost immediately.

"Please go back to bed. I'm only going to the bathroom." I said and with a sigh of relief they went back to bed. They both work very hard and I was mortified that I had disturbed their sleep.

The next day I woke about ten in the morning. Everyone was elsewhere in the house. They didn't hear me get up. I made my way to the kitchen. I started to prepare some toast and coffee for myself. When I turned and started for the table I stopped mid-way with a mug of coffee and a plate in my left hand. I saw my son-in-law standing about half way down the stairs. He had the look of absolute terror on his face. He started yelling "Honey come quick your mother is making toast!" my daughter descended the stairs flying past him at the speed of light. She took me by my good arm removing my mug of coffee and the plate. She led me to a chair at the table.

"Mother! Mother! Please sit here, please." She said as if she was speaking to a child. She then proceeded to finish the toast and coffee preparation I was doing. "Please don't move until I'm done." She was so insistent that I dared not move at all. The thought occurred to me that maybe I should ask for permission to eat after she placed it in front of me. I stopped myself not wanting to anger her or cause her any discomfort. I knew that she and her hubby only meant well.

Three days had passed when that old saying about guests and fish came into my mind. I had watched so many kid shows that I was feeling as if my brain was turning into corn chowder. 'Pretty, Pretty Pony' and 'Happy Bunny' were on at least five times a day as well as 'The Sword and the Dragon' and "King of the Hill'. When my daughter took my grandson to his music class, I asked little Abby if she would like to see one of my shows.

The show is called 'Here Comes the Bride' and she became hooked on it immediately. It's about young women going through the process of choosing a wedding gown. The little kid was so taken by the program that she decided that we would have to design our own dresses. We made every style of bride dress that could possibly be created. We watched the show nonstop for a day and evening. Little Abby said, "We need to put all our brides into a book and I will write the words for it with the help of my mommy. It will be called 'How Brides Have Babies'".

I was rolling in laughter while my daughter stood by clearly not amused. I couldn't wait to hear this story. While my daughter wrote, her little darling dictated. It was a good story and quite tame, I might add, when compared with its title. The story was about a boy and a girl meeting, falling in love, getting married and then having a baby. It was about two and a half paragraphs long and very cute. When the book was completed the little author was very pleased.

I worried more and more about my patients with the passing of time away from the five homes I cover for Dr. Big Guy. Leda was covering them for me. Dr. Seal was taking all of my calls and seeing my patients in the office, but only those that needed immediate attention. She was not pleased with my absence and she complained that I had been gone too long. It had been less than five days. "What the hell is going on? Where the hell have you been and why haven't you been at work?" Dr. Big yelled when I answered my cell phone.

"While you were on vacation, I fell outside the office door and broken my arm, if you remember. I am told I may not be able to use it again." I replied.

"I come and get you, drive you to nursing home so you can make your rounds." He demanded. How very big of him I thought to myself.

"I don't think I can do that I'm seeing another specialist in the morning. I will let you know if he releases me to return to work or if the break in the arm will require surgery." I said calmly.

"Surgery! Why the hell would you need surgery!" he yells again.

"Well there was a lot of ice in front of the office door. I have a bad fracture of my arm." I told him.

"Oh I see" he replied more calmly. I think he was beginning to see, that perhaps, dollar signs may be involved. The last thing on my mind was any type of monetary claim, although my lawyer would have much to say on this when I told him what had happened to me. He wanted to file a claim right away but I refused. It wasn't anyone's fault as far as I was concerned .It was only an act of God, Nature and one of the draw backs of living in the Midwest.

The next day I discovered that I had met my match in the new orthopedic surgeon. Dr. Walker was as gruff and out spoken as I. He had reddish hair, freckles and big blue eyes. "Well I think your arm is going to be ok, lady. Look at mine." He said holding his right arm up bending and straightening it. "I did it skiing and I know I don't have total range with it but it is good enough for me to still practice and do surgery. I think you are going to get the same result if we use our heads here and treat this very conservatively." He went to work removing the large white cast that had me waving at everyone. He took more x-rays and then replaced it with a more practical one that allowed me to have my arm down in a semi-bent position. "So what's your favorite color?" he asked.

"Purple." I replied and as I looked down at my arm the cast turned that bright hue.

"Well I thought so and that's why I picked it for you." He said smiling. "There is nothing I can do about the bone that is broken off completely. If we leave this cast on for about two weeks and then get you some therapy, I think you will regain about sixty percent of the use of it back. Now you have to be careful because you could easily dislocate it again."

"I will have to do some minor suturing, pap smears, cleaning out ears and some casting and ace wrapping myself Doctor. Will I be able to do those things again?" I asked.

"Don't you worry about a damned thing, lady I think you will be pleased with the outcome. Just give it some time." He replied.

"When can I go back to work?" I asked.

"Go back anytime you want and I will see you in two weeks. The nurse has all your paperwork ready for you." He said as he left the room.

I couldn't keep Dr. Big Guy waiting any longer, I returned to work in the next morning. My son-in-law reluctantly gave me back my car keys. While he didn't like the thought of me being there day in and day out, he thought me totally incapable of handling my own affairs, let alone driving myself around with a cast on one arm. He was really freaked out. I knew he had my best interest at heart. I knew, also, that he didn't want me as a permanent resident in his home should I wreck my car and or myself. I fully understand him now and then. I like living alone and enjoy doing my own thing.

Off I went driving with one arm. That wasn't so bad but as soon as Dr. Big got the news, he had the service give me all the calls for my five nursing homes. It became a real challenge as I didn't have a hands free device to answer the phone in my car without taking my one hand off the wheel. Every time the phone rang, I had to pull off the road in order to answer it. I would have to pull back into traffic after I was finished with the call causing a lot of time to be wasted.

The dilemma caused me to be late for a meeting one night. My tardiness made Dr. Big Guy very angry. He had planned the meeting with many other health care providers and Doctors. Even though I was very late all the other doctors stayed to greet me. They all wanted to talk to me about old times and what I was now doing. They wanted to know what had happened to my arm. They were people I had worked with over the years that knew me, knew my work skills and abilities. Dr. Big doesn't like to share the spot light with anyone else. He let me know that it was time to leave. I think he was trying to impress me that night with his vast knowledge and influence over the medical community in the area. I don't think he realized that since I was so much older than he, I would know all the health care providers in the area. The fact that I held their respect put him out of sorts.

The whole parking lot was a sheet of ice as I walked to my car that night trying not to fall again. It was very cold and the wind blew hard. I couldn't believe I parked so far away but the parking lot was full when I had arrived. I could hear Dr. Big Guy's tires squealing as he pulled out of the lot in his sports car. I took a deep breath of relief when I got in my car and slowly drove home.

Over the next few weeks I did fairly well driving myself around with one arm. I was getting to all of my nursing homes. I was able to assess the patients and do the work with a little extra effort on my part. I felt very proud I could do all of it. The patients loved my purple cast. They told me how glad they were I was back with them again. My medical assistant at Dr. Nelson's office helped me devised a way to do a one armed pap smear. I always marveled at the handicapped when seeing how they got around. I was getting a taste of their real world, a world very hard and trying. I knew there was no comparison of my temporary affliction and that of a wheelchair bound or bed bound person. There is no escape for the permanently handicapped. The ability of those individuals to adapt and manage their lives is a gift from God. Seeing them made me more determined than ever to get the use of my arm back.

I couldn't wait for the cast to come off! It itched so badly. I had various things I put down it so I could scratch my arm. My favorite was a long oversized emery board that worked well. But when the cast finally came off I found that I could only move my arm about thirty degrees. I was disappointed and worried that this may be a permanent state for me. My friend and associate, Rick, was a physical therapist whom I had known for many years. I had referred most of my patients to him for therapy. Late one day, he came bursting into my office. "I'm going to do your therapy myself!" he commanded.

"But you can't, Rick, I have HMO insurance and I have to go where they tell me to go." I replied.

"Nonsense! You will come to my office and I will do it for you, for free. It is the least I can do for you after all the patients you have referred to me over the years." He said. "I won't hear of you going elsewhere. It's all settled, three times a week in my office." He left me sitting there with my mouth gaping open as he walked out. I understood this kind of friendship to be priceless and rare. I wanted to cry but before I could even respond to my feelings, I was being called into a room to see my next patient. Within three weeks Rick had my arm back to almost full range of motion. I was able to wash my face and comb my hair using both hands again. When I returned to the HMO clinic to see Dr. Walker for my follow up visit, he was very impressed.

"I just knew I was right! I knew a conservative approach would work and preserve the arms many functions. I want all the other Docs here to see this. You wait right here while I go and get them." He said, very excited and left the room. In minutes the room was full of doctors and other nurses all taking turns examining my arm. As they were patting Dr. Walker on the back and listening to him telling them how he did it, I slipped from the room and returned to my own office.

No one in the office but the medical assistant who worked with me noticed that the purple cast was gone. It was more than a month before Dr. Big noticed anything. "What happened to your cast? I thought you said your arm was permanently damaged?" he asked.

"I've been going to therapy for the past month. I have worked hard to regain almost full range of motion." I replied.

"See, I knew you were overreacting and making it a big thing for nothing! Your numbers have slipped over the last month so get busy and bring them up. I can't continue to keep two nurse practitioners here." He said and walked from the room. I knew that Leda saw less than half the patients I saw on any given day. She came to work whenever she wanted. I knew this to be true because I asked her one day when she arrived at the office at two in the afternoon looking as if she had just rolled out of bed and decided to come to work.

"Oh I haven't seen anyone yet. I just got here." She told me. I started to mark the days off on my calendar toward a retirement date.

Chapter 8

Breaking Up Is Hard To Do

Spring was soon to become summer and I needed to start telling everyone that I plan to retire in about three or four months. My older daughter was already making plans for me. She wanted me to stay with her family and be a live-in babysitter for the children so she could go back to work. She is a very bright woman. I know she wants to return to her career. She has three children she home schools. Home schooling was not what I had in mind for my retirement but I would have to cross that bridge later.

I started to tell many of my patients that I had been caring for these many years that I may soon retire. "But you're not old enough." Mr. Davis said when I broke the news to him. When I told him my age he was shocked to hear it. When I look in the mirror, I see an old woman looking back at me. I don't know what patients like Mr. Davis see when they look at me. My guess is that they don't think much about me at all. Most people don't care who gives them their health care as long as their needs are met in an efficient and pleasant manner that doesn't cost too much. Health care can be delivered by an ape for all they care.

Things seemed to be getting harder for me. Days got longer and went by much slower than at any other time in my life. I started having dreams of being at home not knowing what to do with my time. I had dreams of not having enough money to live. In my dreams I have to find some other type of work. In one dream I am actually begging at the door of a church for heaven sakes. I woke and realized that it was only a dream. I can't seem to get through my days any quicker. I guess that lack of good sleep made the days drag on and on. It took me longer to get to all my homes and see all of my patients. Even as I began to slow down, I started to think that maybe I made the wrong decision.

One night I woke in a cold sweat. I was shaking as if I had a fever. Then I remembered the dream I just had. A man that looked a lot like Dr. Big was talking to me in that dream. What he said was most disturbing to recall. "You are a coward! You are turning your back on the very people that depend on you every day. What good are you if you can't help them? Why are you running away?" When I awakened fully, I realized that it wasn't Dr. Big Guy at all! It was my own conscience that was talking to me. It was true I was deserting the people in my care. I was leaving them behind. I was expecting them to find other means of health care and other ways of dealing with their illnesses. There it was that old fashioned guilt I learned to take on as a child. I've even learned to pass it on to my daughters.

Growing up in the forties and fifties, the guilt card was played almost daily by my parents, teachers and clergy. In many ways guilt served us well for generations. "If you don't study you will grow up dumb and you won't get a job. You will be a burden on your family and cause them shame." This was the constant plea from my parents every report card period of the school year. I was guilty and got a steady dose of guilt served to me every day.

I did the same to my daughters "If you misbehave people will say it is because you come from a broken home." I was a single mother and raised my girls alone from the time they were born, almost. "You can't go out looking like that; people will say it is because your mother can't take proper care of you because she is working all the time." I said these things whenever my girls did something or wore something that didn't meet with my approval. I passed on the same guilt to a new generation.

Analyzing my situation, I saw that I was guilty of many things. I was guilty because I was deserting my patients. I was a coward because I couldn't handle the pressure of the job anymore. I couldn't change the situation for the people in my care in those appalling living conditions. When it came down to the facts, what was it that I did for them anyway? I ordered pills for them, an IV or a test of some kind. I gave them a little kindness and comfort in time of need, these were small and very insignificant things. I realized that I can change nothing for them at all. I'm guilty of thinking I'm so powerful that only I can care for them, another big sin. No one person on this earth is that important to anyone else. If I leave, I admit that I am no good to anyone anymore. I realized that I needed my patients as much, if not more, than they need me. Without them I would have to seek another identity. I would no longer be Miss Mary the health care provider. Who would I be? I would have to find out very soon when I won't be there to give comfort or pills. It occurred to me that after I'm gone in a few weeks no one will even remember that I was there and did anything.

Such revelation started me thinking about all the things I have experienced in my nearly fifty years as a nurse and nurse practitioner. I could write a book, like everyone has been telling me I must. But I really am a coward. I couldn't see myself writing some sort of tell-all exposé. If I tried to go to the state with all of the bizarre incidents that have taken place in the homes where the elderly are supposed to be taken care of I would have to have proof. I would need witnesses, documentation, and pictures to back my stories. I would have had to record facts, times, dates and names of people and places. Slowly the idea came to me that I could, however, write a memoir based on my experiences. A memoir can admit many truths without the penalty of having to explain anything. Someone once said that when you write a biography or other works of nonfiction you can lie like hell but when you write a novel or a memoir, you are free to tell the truth.

The biggest problem looming for me was telling Dr. Big Guy of my plans to leave him. I knew he would not be happy because I worked about 80 hours a week. I am on call twenty-four hours a day, every day. He would know that this would mean he would have to do all of my work as well as his own until he found a replacement for me. Finding someone to work all those hours is not likely as most nurse practitioners are female, wives and mothers. Most are unwilling and or would find it difficult to put in that many hours in one week.

Julia Fallon and I met for dinner one evening to discuss my new plans. She is a fellow nurse practitioner who is always very objective in her view of things. I like to bounce ideas off her when I can. We met many years ago when she was a new graduate. She came to work on my floor at the hospital. She is very intelligent and insightful. "He can fire you. You know that don't you." She said over her glass of wine. "This is an 'at will' state and if an employer wants to let you go he doesn't have to have a good reason for doing it."

"Oh he wouldn't do that!" I reply, looking up at her from my rib eye steak dinner. Looking up is what I really have to do to see her. Julia is very tall, has a full head of reddish curly hair and bright blue eyes. She has a commanding presence where ever she goes. She has a great sense of humor and can see the comedic side in everything. When I tell her some of the things the nursing home staff members say to me she always ends up rolling in laughter at every incident while I sit there crying with my sad face about to fall into my soup.

"From what you've told me about him, oh yes, I think Dr. Big would indeed send you packing!" she informs me. "I would give him only two or three weeks' notice if I were you." She is saying this but I can't believe it. "Do you get a vacation? Take a vacation and go somewhere, rest up. Then come back and tell him."

"So what do you think about my writing a memoir about all my experiences?" I ask, as much to change the subject as to get her opinion on the matter. She has told me, many times, I need to do this. But I know those times were only during gab fests for entertainment. I really wanted her input on the subject. I wanted some real advice and answers.

"I can't wait to read it! All of you stories are so funny. I will be splitting my sides at the turn of very page! When will the first book come out?" she asks.

"Excuse me, the first book? What makes you think I can write more than one?" I want to know.

"Oh you will write more than one, which my dear, is for certain." She replied with unwavering conviction. When we left the restaurant, I knew that Julia has given me a lot to think about, as always. So I put the breaking up plan aside for another month or two. I guessed it can't hurt. Can it?

Chapter 9

The Coward Finds Courage

"I want you to see what real courage is, instead of getting the idea that courage is a man with a gun in his hand. It's when you know you're licked before you begin, but you begin anyway and you see it through no matter what."

Atticus Finch, From Haper Lee's
To Kill A Mockingbird

The long hot summer drags on. The month of September has almost arrived with days that are equally as hot and sunny as the previous months. Fall shows no sign of coming. I have word from social security. They send me a letter at least very three days or so with more rules and different quotes on how much money I will receive from them each month. Every letter tells me that I cannot work after the thirty-first of October. If I work past that date I will forfeit my December payment.

I have requested three weeks' vacation starting the second week in October. Now that it has been approved I have asked for a meeting with Dr. Big Guy for next week. I plan to tell him that I will be retiring so if he fires me I will be able to go on the spot without a problem. I think it was good advice from Julia Fallon to wait. I can't give only two or three weeks' notice so I will be giving about five weeks which I feel is reasonable.

I have cherished the last few months with my patients. They seem to sense that a change is coming. I have told many of them that I see in the office that I will be leaving but in the nursing homes, it is different. I can't bring myself to do it. I have hinted to some of the staff that I am now full retirement age. The good ones express their concern for my possible departure. The administration, however, I am sure are counting the days on their calendars as am I.

With the vacation time I requested approved and my meeting with Dr. Big all set for next week, I am ready to start my day. I just need that courage and a big cup of morning Joe to get going. An old country gospel tune is playing as I pull into my spot at the nursing home. "On the wings of a snow white Dove He sends His pure sweet love, a sign from above on the wings of a dove. When trouble surrounds us, when evil comes He sends down His love on the wings of a dove." I have always liked that tune even when it isn't being sung on a Sunday morning.

The same old smell of heat, food, human waste and flowers hits me as I get out of the car. That smell I will never be able to forget, no matter where I go or what I do after I am gone. The staff at Whispering Pines started coming to me with tears in their eyes asking me to take them with me where ever it is that I am going. "I'm not leaving to go elsewhere! I'm going to retire. I hope sooner rather than later. I have no job for any of you." I tell them. I feel touched and sad all at the same time. I really wish I did have the power that they seem to think I hold to help them.

"Oh, you could start your own nursing home, Miss Mary", pleaded Mrs. Martin. "You smart and you got money too." The money part they sure had wrong. The smart part, well I'm not banking on that either. It is very difficult to get approval from the state to open a nursing home. It has to go to the legislature for a certificate of need. I would need to have a medical doctor as a partner due to the way the laws are set up. In this state a nurse or nurse practitioner is not allowed to own a nursing home. I had talked with lots of health care administrators who would love to work with me on such a venture. If I was a younger woman or even had money to invest, I would consider it. There are more elderly people living today than any other time in our history. Every day at least ten thousand people turn sixty-five years old here in the United States. When I started out in nursing, I was too busy trying to raise a family and keep a roof over our heads to consider any business arrangement. Most homes today are owned by large companies who are interested in turning a profit. They are not necessarily thinking about delivering good health care as it is very costly. I didn't have the courage then to venture into business and I know I don't possess it now. Dreams are the stuff of which reality is made. I sometimes dream of doing just that, having my own nursing home. I fantasize about hiring all the good people I know I can trust to do the job right. But as I approach the end of my career, I know it will never come to pass. I can't spend even a minute looking back on my life and thinking what if I had done this or that. It just isn't a good thing to do.

I remember my first encounter with nursing home patients. I was nineteen years old and living the life of a privileged kid. I had graduated high school and was unable to find a job. I was dating a lot back then but that term "dating" meant something entirely different than it does in today's world. Back then a boy would ask you to go to a movie, roller skating, bowling or to a football game. You would go out for a coke or a hamburger and you would be home at the appointed time. Even a good night kiss was never mentioned until at least the third date if you were known as a "Nice Girl". Dating in today's world means that you are having sex. I think it is sad the kind of dating we did back then is gone. It was a time to get to know people in a more meaningful way. You got to know what they liked and didn't like. You learned how to behave and what was expected of you in a relationship. I'm not saying that there wasn't a lot of sex going on back then. I know that it happened all the time. Mostly it occurred between couples that had been steady dating for a long time and planning to marry in the near future. I knew that it happened in other situations as well but it was less talked about.

Staying out until midnight or one in the morning was common for me back then and I would sleep late. I did whatever I had to do around the house to help my mother. I was pretty much a night owl even then. On a cool morning in late August I was sleeping in as usual when I was awakened by my father. "You no sleep all day." He said in his broken English. "You get dressed and you come with me."

"Where are we going Pa?" I asked but he did not answer. He often called on me to go to the city with him. I would help deliver produce from our gardens to individuals and small businesses who purchased these goods from our farm. When I climbed into the car I was surprised to see that there were no fruits or vegetables for market. I saw the large white envelop that I kept my high school diploma and my letter of recommendation from my teacher Miss Wilhelm. I couldn't fathom why it was on the front seat of the car. My father was a man with a very short fuse so I knew better than to ask again where we might be headed.

We hadn't gone very far down the big highway, less than ten miles, when my father turned onto the little road that led to the Great Maple Tree Nursing and Rest Home. I knew the place well; it had been the chicken coop of a large farm in that area of the county. I had already been there and had put in an application for a job as a secretary or a receptionist. But I was told that there was no such position available. "Mrs. Dunn she wants to see us." Pa said as we entered. We were shown to a small room off the main office. We waited there as my father twirled his hat in his hands.

A small woman with gray hair dressed in a starched white uniform with a high collar and three quarter length sleeves entered the room. She was wearing a large white nurse's cap with a black stipe on it. She wore orthopedic shoes with white stockings. A small gray haired man followed her into the room. He wore brown dress pants and a white shirt without a tie and opened at the neck. "Miss Rosario, I'm Mrs. Dunn and this is my husband." She said waving a hand at him but not allowing him to speak. She looked me up and down as if she were purchasing livestock. "I guess you're kind of puny aren't you? Well you have this and this is golden." She said as she took the diploma from me along with my letter from Miss Wilhelm. She was my teacher in high school and she wrote these letters for all the girls in her secretarial classes. "I don't have need of a secretary but I do need a good nurse's aide. I think I can turn you into one. If you are willing to work hard, I can teach you everything you need to know to work here." I was stunned and could think of nothing to say but I nodded my head in agreement. I had a job at Mrs. Dunn's nursing and rest home making one dollar an hour.

For the first few weeks I met with Mrs. Dunn in the class room she had upstairs in the home. She proceeded to teach me all I needed to know in order to work there. I took to the job like a duck to water. I liked old people, after all, my father was seventy and my mother was fifty-four. All of their friends from the old country were all about the same age. I was pretty used to spending a lot of time with people who could have been my grandparents.

Mrs. Dunn was the first person to ever believe that I could be anything other than a skinny little girl without the brain with which she was born. She taught and encouraged me to learn something new about life and health care every day. I have been forever grateful to her for her faith in me and my abilities. She instilled in me the love of the elderly who have so much to offer us if we just listen to them.

I wish, even today, they were not tucked away in facilities and removed from society. Their stories and experiences could go a long way in helping us understand the world we live in and how we got to where we are today. They could teach us a lot. The world today is all about the young. The whole of advertising is done to the population between the ages of eighteen and twenty-nine and perhaps even younger. The rest of us just have to try and figure out what it is they want us to know or buy.

If it hadn't been for that first job and the elderly there in that first nursing home, I doubt I would have become a nurse or a nurse practitioner. If it wasn't for the elderly no president would ever get elected to office. The drug companies would not exist as the multi-billion dollar entities they are today. Millions of small things we do every day have been handed down to us by the previous generations. What was once old is new again and again if we care to look back and find it.

Those words of Harper Lee, one of my favorite authors, I try to internalize every day of my life as the clock is winding down. If we keep doing the things we believe in we may eventually get others to believe in them.

Chapter 10

Pleasant Persona Without Passion

A film director named John Boorman once said, and I don't know why I remember it. "What is passion? It is surely the becoming of a person...........In passion, the body and the spirit seek expression......The more unbearable does life seem without it. It reminds us that if passion dies or is denied, we are partly dead and, that soon, come what may, we will be wholly so."

Pleasant and calm no matter what is the disposition I'm tried to maintain as I went about my duties. I tried to be a no drama mama just like President and Mrs. Obama. In that frame of mind everything seemed to be ok with me as I started my new week. No fires and no explosions between me and Dr. Big had occurred in about three days. I guessed maybe he's not entirely a sanctimonious beast of a man doctor. I contemplated the meeting with him set for the end of the week, confident that it would go well. I tried to think positively that he would wish me a happy retirement.

The new serenity lasted a little over twenty-four hours. It began to erode on Tuesday afternoon during office hours. At one o'clock I had completed my morning office hours. The afternoon was supposed to be spent catching up on paper work, filling out forms, reading e-mails and responding to them. It is also a time for refilling medication requests from the pharmacies.

Leda was, once again, out of town or unavailable for reasons unknown. I had just been informed that I was covering for her. She is quite the party girl. She, Dr. Big Guy and the young girls who worked in the office went out a lot to night clubs as do all the young.

The receptionist buzzed me and told me that a phone call was holding for me on line one. "It is a nursing home called Hampton Cove, they want to know something about a medication order."

"Thank you, Victoria," I replied and I pick up line one. "This is Mary, how may I help you?" "am lookin for Leda!" says a strong male voice on the other end.

"Well I'm covering for Leda. She is unavailable at this time. How may I assist you?" I asked.

"Well we finally got a IV into this here patient Mr. Calhoun and am bout to hang them piggy back IV antibiotics of his. His IV been out for three days and I got the IV company to come put a line in him." said the strong male voice. It meant that the patient had a central line in the large vein in his upper arm. A piggy back is a small bag of fluid containing medication that can be plugged into a main IV or hooked in directly to it.

"Ok to whom am I speaking?" I asked in a cheerful voice.

"This is Jay-Jay. I is the nurse on this here floor at Hampton Cove. Izz just letin you know that I got six of these here bags of antibiotics to hang on this IV for Mr. Calhoun. I think I can get them all in if I hang them one after the other and run them at full speed." He said. The little bags of medication are very durable and medications in them can stay fresh for quite some time.

That pleasant calm I had been maintaining for the last twenty-four hours flowed away as I listened. I wondered how in God's name one could be so void of any common sense what so ever. I thought I had heard it all. I thought nothing could have shaken my new found serenity, but I was wrong. I realized there just is no end to some people's stupidity!

I took a deep breath and tried to calm and steady my voice as I replied "Well that is not a good idea to do it that way. You may be able to complete all the IV's but the patient will be dead. You will need to just retime all of those bags and change the dates on them."

"What you mean girl! I ain't got time for that, I got to get out of here on time today after my shift is over." he yelled into the phone. "I don't know what you talking about!"

Please sir," I replied. "Let me talk to your supervisor then she can help you with this."

"I ain't letting you talk to nobody lady! You ain't getting me into no trouble!" I pulled the phone from my ear quickly as he banged it down hard.

There was only one thing for me to do. I ran into Dr. Big Guy's office. He was sitting with his feet up on his desk dictating notes into a small recorder. He was well dressed again that day and I'm sure he was planning a night out at his club. "Excuse me, sir, but can you tell me how to get to Hampton Cove? I have to get there before the nurse kills a patient!" I exclaimed.

"What the hell are you talking about?" he asked as he released the recorder button and set it down on his desk. I explained the phone call I had received from Jay-Jay at Hampton Cove. Dr. Big just started to chuckle and said, "oh come on, no one would do that. He is just pulling the leg." His understanding of American slang was always interesting to say the least.

I left the office running. It wasn't pretty seeing a fat old woman run. I'm wide, round and built close to the ground, if you get my meaning. To say that I'm vertically challenged is putting it mildly. Hampton Cove is about twenty miles from our office. For some reason there was a lot of traffic on the highway. I started out going about eighty miles per hour but I had to drop my speed. Then I saw there was construction on that avenue. I thought, oh no I'll never get there in time before Jay-Jay gives Mr. Calhoun an over dose of medication! Luck was on my side because there wasn't a lot of truck traffic on the highway. There was only a bunch of small foreign cars. I swung the big town car on to the shoulder of the road and hit the gas passing them all as if they were at a standstill. I prayed that there were no police around. In about fifteen minutes I saw the parking lot of Hampton Cove on my left. I swerved the car into it at breakneck speed.

It was supposed to be one of those places that offer sub-acute care to patients. That is, the patients are still pretty sick when they are admitted but they no longer need to be in the hospital. They are sent there to finish receiving long term antibiotics, physical therapy and follow up testing. If the person is lucky to survive that specialized care, they may get to go home.

One whiff of the air as I got out of the car told me that The Hamptons, as Leda called it, was no different from any other nursing facility in the area. It is poorly staffed and poorly maintained. I didn't know my way around the place so I had to find the supervisor and get to Mr. Calhoun before it was too late. The front desk person rang her for me. After what seemed to me like an incredibly long time, I saw her slowly coming down the hall. She was so large that she had difficulty passing through the doorway! I introduced myself, explained who I was and why I had come. Sweat was pouring down her face and it was actually dripping onto the floor at her feet.

Seeing the expression on my face she said, "No air conditioning here." Breathing heavily, she led me down a long hallway to the sub-acute unit. We found Jay-Jay and I calmly retimed and dated all of the IV antibiotics as he stood over me with a scalding expression on his face.

"Now Jay-Jay," I explained calmly as I could. "Hang one of these bags every six hours until the three week therapy is completed." I went to see Mr. Calhoun who turned out to be a very thin, blind and bedridden black man. He was very sick. I assured Jay-Jay that Leda would return soon. She would be here to follow up on the care of the patient.

The supervisor had been standing there the whole time waiting for me to finish. Then she insisted on walking me out to my car. "You really don't have to Mrs. Buckley. I can find my way out." I said.

"Oh it's no trouble at all." She said smiling broadly. She had a towel around her neck to catch the sweat. I followed her down the hall. She talked on and on in a pleasant voice as she accompanied me. "There was a time when I wanted to become a nurse practitioner in the worst way. I was raising a family then. I could never find the time or the money to do it." I, once again, had to thank God that I was fortunate enough to have worked in a facility that had a Tuition reimbursement program. I had taken advantage of it at that time. I felt bad for Mrs. Buckley because she seemed like a nice individual who may have made a good practitioner.

When I got in my car I could feel the serenity returning. As I drove back to the office, the calm may have returned, but the passion, I was sure, would never die, no matter how hard I tried to suppress it. Thank you, Mr. Boorman, for your very wise words.

Chapter 11

Oh, How I Have Waited For This Day!

It seemed as if Friday would never come. Maybe I was wishing it wouldn't. It is hard not to like a bright sunny day. A song called "You're the reason I don't sleep at night" is playing on my CD in the car. It's very appropriate because I haven't slept much all week. The reason was, not only double the call as Leda was still out of town or otherwise still unavailable, I worried what Dr. Big Guy's reaction. What would he have to say today when I meet with him to tell him my retirement plans? I had the car windows down as I cruised at the speed limit that morning. A guy in a car in the lane next to me had his window down too. I noticed he was holding a pair of white underwear out his driver's side window! If you're reading this book, I know what you're thinking. I assure you that I cannot make this stuff up. I'm really not that creative. I don't know why he was flying his fruit of the looms out the window! Perhaps, he didn't have a quarter for the dryer at the Laundromat or the time to go there and dry them properly. I blew the horn lightly as I pass him. He waved and smiled at me.

I wanted the day to go well and to go fast. Taking a deep breath, I asked God to help me remain calm and in control. I had worked almost fifty years for that day. I hoped to handle a few more hours. I breezed through rounds at Whispering Pines and Sunny Side. The girls at the Pines gave me a beautiful bunch of flowers and a card they all signed. "Just in case you don't come back after today, we want you to know that we will miss you," Mrs. Martin said. I was surprised they hadn't leaked my plans to Dr. Big Guy. I was very touched. My eyes filled with tears as they all lined up to give me hugs.

While things there were far from perfect and smelled very bad, I noticed they had made some improvements. Since I came there, the fall rate or the number of patients that fell or got injuries, dropped considerablely. They started a program that allows them to have one on one care givers for those patients who were always falling or otherwise getting hurt. Even Elmer, Mr. Pee in the water fountain, has someone with him. The people assigned to our frequent fallers were health aides in training to be occupational therapy assistants. They needed to put in a set number of hours before getting their certification as a trained health aide. It was not a permanent solution but at any rate, it made things better.

At Sunny Side Nursing Home Johanna looked a little down. "I'm just not getting the support I need here from the staff and administration to do this job. When you go, I will have no one to help me. Can't you ask Dr. Big Guy to take me on after you leave?" Her green eyes sparkled as she looked a little more hopeful.

"Well, I don't think it would hurt to ask him" I reply not knowing if he would consider it. "I will put in a word with him that you're looking for an office based practice. You will have to call him yourself and let him know you're interested."

Carroll Square was on my way back to the office, so I stopped there because I received a call from my favorite nurse. Princess called to say that Toya, a thirty-three year old woman with advanced HIV/Aids wouldn't take her antiviral drugs. Princess was a great nurse even though she was only a practical nurse. "Why is she still there?" I demand. "I told the night nurse to send her back to the hospital as she will die without those medications. Get her to sign a release of responsibility or a DNR or consent for Hospice or something."

"I don't know why she won't take them, Miss Mary; I try so hard with her. When she's in the hospital she does just fine." She replies with concern in her voice.

"I know you do, Princess and I appreciate all your efforts, but she must be sent at once!" I am trying my calm voice.

"I don't think them administrators going to let her go this time. The super is here and she says 'don't send her no more'." Princess said.

I headed right for Toya's room when I arrived. I was always amazed they make such an effort to keep this place clean even though it is such a dump. My pleading with Toya to take her meds is no more successful than Princess's. I was frustrated and worried that this young girl would surely lose her life soon. I wrote orders to transfer the patient to the hospital immediately. It was getting late and I had to hurry to get to the office for my office hours. I didn't want the meeting with Dr. Big Guy to be delayed in any way.

The entire staff was assembled in the waiting room when I arrive. Dr. Big Guy had called a general meeting of all staff. Oh no! I thought to myself, this is not going to go well. Our eyes met and he said, "Take a seat; I'll deal with you later." The meeting, which was a whole lot about nothing in particular, went on for two hours. I think he just liked the adoration he received in these, so call, staff meetings as well as the sound of his own voice.

The office hours started late and every fifteen minute slot was filled. Patients were trying to get in to see me before I retired. I had quietly informed a lot of my regular people I had been seeing for many years. I would miss them very much. Medical practice afforded me many intimate, yet professional, relationships with different types of people from lawyers, doctors, and teachers to business people and engineers. I saw waitresses, truck drivers, gardeners and retail workers. I saw those who made minimum wage as well as those on public assistance who can't earn their own way. I had come to value them all. I felt the weight of the privilege it was to care for them. I needed that heady feeling it gave me that they trusted me with their lives. I hoped when I was working just one day a week it would be enough to fill the need. I prayed they would be just as content with their new health care provider.

It was seven o'clock when Dr. Big finally called me into his office. Dr. Seal was also present. She would need to be aware of my plans. "So what is on the mind?" He began with another attempt at

English language slang. (He was born and raised in the Middle East but his medical education took place here in the United States.)

"Well," I began. "I'm glad that Dr. Seal has joined us as what I have to say concerns her also. I would like to inform you that I wish to retire. I am tendering my resignation effective five weeks from today. I want to thank you both for giving me the opportunity to have been in your employ." I thought the little speech sounded quite calm and very professional as I handed them each a copy of my letter of termination/retirement from their practice.

"Oh do not be silly!" Replied Dr. Big Guy as he tosses the paper onto his desk. "You are tired. Take your vacation and return in a few weeks. We will cover you." I mentally noted that my leaving wasn't sinking into him. He would never take me seriously even if I stay at work until one hundred years old!

"I have confirmed my retirement date with social security and Medicare." I reply firmly.

He jumped to his feet "That does not mean that you cannot work." He starts pacing back and forth. "Tree! Tree!" he yelled, holding up three fingers of his right hand, thumb, index and middle fingers, shoving them in my face. "I give you tree nursing home that is all, you can take your time with them. Go there when you want to go. You don't have to work hard as you do. I have never understood why you do all you do anyway."

"It is retirement that I seek, Sir, not more nursing homes with twenty-four hours a day call seven days a week." I said it in the calmest voice I could muster up to explain my feelings and my plans to him. "I don't think you realize that working here has taken its toll on me. My health status is no longer the best. I don't want to be a burden on you or the practice."

"Ha!" he laughs loudly. "You will never be a burden here. Take a month off and come back to work you will feel better and we will put all this nonsense behind us."

Dr. Seal rose and gave me her hand "I wish you the best in whatever you decide to do. It has been a pleasure to have worked with you." She releases my hand and walks from the room. I didn't reply to Dr. Big as it is getting me nowhere.

"Doctor I want to let you know that the nurse practitioner named Johanna at Sunny Side is interested in working for an office based practice. She was wondering if you would be interested in interviewing her for my position." I said hoping he would realize I was serious about retiring.

"I have already hired a friend of Leda's. Her name is Danita and she is to start next week. I hope you will show her the rope." He says. I wanted to laugh at that but I didn't. I wondered why he didn't ask Leda to 'show her the rope' since they were friends. But since she was still out of town or otherwise unavailable I didn't ask.

Night had fallen when I left the office. Clouds had moved in with drizzling rain. The temperature had cooled. I guessed, finally, fall had arrived. I drove home not knowing if I felt relief or regret, maybe a little of both. It is not the elated feeling that I thought I would have after all the agonizing over how to tell Dr. Big of my future plans.

The Jay Leno monologue is well underway when I crawled into bed. My arms and legs felt like lead weights , I drifted off to sleep. My cell phone started to ring. "Miss Mary, it's Princess, I'm workin a double over here at Carroll Square. I need to let you know that Toya just had a cardiac arrest and the paramedics are here working on her." Princess shouts into the phone.

"But I ordered her to return to the hospital today! She was getting pretty sick then when she wouldn't take her meds. Why was she not sent back earlier?" I say with great frustration.

"I know you did, Miss Mary, but they wouldn't let me send her! Look I got to go and do the paperwork." Princess yelled with a shaking voice as she hung up. I was wide awake with no chance sleep. I got up, pace the floor a few times and got a drink of water. Then the phone rang again and it was the answering service.

"Miss Mary, I have Dr. Seal on the other line. She wants to talk to you."

"You may put her through to me Grace and thank you." I replied, realizing she must be on call tonight for Dr. Big Guy who was, most likely out with his young women. Dr. Seal was single, young and she likes to party. But she wasn't too happy about Dr. Big running wild. She thought he should stay with his wife or divorce her.

"Mary your patient was DOA at the emergency room just now. What the hell happened to her?" Dr. Seal demands.

"Dr. Seal she had advanced HIV/AIDS and she was not taking her meds. She had been refusing them. I told them at the home to send her back to hospital earlier today when she was showing signs of failure then but they wouldn't do it. All of my orders are there on the chart you can go there and read them if you like." I replied.

"I don't need to do that, I believe you. I don't know why Big Guy puts up with those places. I, for one, will not be caught dead in any of them. He better not think that when you leave he can make me start going to nursing homes." She tells me firmly.

After I hang up with Dr. Seal, I just can't sleep. I feel bad about young Toya. There had been so many advances in the treatment of HIV/AIDS. The girl could have done well if she had just taken the meds. I didn't know what her reasons were for refusing them. Perhaps she just wanted to die or thought she would be sent to live at home if she didn't take the meds. No one would ever know the answer.

Chapter 12

The Power And Meaning Of Words

Some people are what you might call plain talkers. They say what they mean and mean what they say. I have always considered myself one of those people. When I hear those in the corporate world using different words to mean something different than what they mean to say, it is a thing I just can't tolerate in any given situation.

However, straight talk used to get me into a lot of trouble. That was how I came to lose Pleasantville and why Leda was brought in to replace me.

About ten years ago there was a state wide investigation of all nursing homes and rehab centers. Certain things were never supposed to happen in these facilities. If such problems did arise, the place would be closed immediately, investigated and eventually, permanently shut down. These things that were never to occur under any circumstances were called 'seminal events'. It was determined that if a patient became dehydrated or was found to have a fecal impaction of the bowel, these health problems are considered preventable. The home is considered negligent in allowing them to occur thus terming them 'a seminal event'. If the home was found to have let any of these types of problem occur they must assume the liability for the cost of them as well. If a patient was found non-responsive with his or her head caught in the side rail of the bed, it was a big red flag that would warrant a full investigation and possible closure of a facility.

Logic would dictate that facilities would monitor the residents for any sort of occurrence and take great care to prevent them from ever happening so no seminal event would ever be reported in any facility. The reality is that preventive care comes at a very high price that most facilities are unwilling to pay. The path taken to prevent such things is to avoid reporting them. Certain words are never allowed to be used in the facility under any circumstances. Instead of preventing seminal events, the home makes it imperative that you, as a health care provider in the facility, never ever use any of these terms that would describe seminal events.

The way this is done is quite simple really. As a health care provider I am forbidden to ever use these terms or words to describe a patient's present or past condition. I can no longer say a patient is dehydrated. I must say that he or she is volume depleted which is also known as hypovolemia. I can also say that the patient has adult onset failure to thrive which means they are suffering from malnutrition. These are acceptable terms and will not bring the state health department running to conduct a full investigation and possible closure of the facility.

Side rails are considered restraints. In this state, facilities are not allowed to restrain patients. Only under the most controlled circumstances is this ever allowed to take place. The patient or patients in question must be deemed a danger to themselves or others. If indeed this is the case the patient must be placed on one to one care. The restraints have to be agreed upon by the guardian, family member or the patient (if he is able), before they can be used. This agreement must be in writing and signed by all parties involved. The restraints must be checked every fifteen minutes and documented that they are in place and causing no harm to the patient's skin, bones or circulation etc. They must be made for ease of removal in case of a fire or other disaster. In this state, there is a law stating a patient has a right to fall. If, however, a broken hip or some other injury occurs, the facility is responsible and must pay for the care of the patient for the injury sustained. Neither the patient nor his or her insurance company is liable for the expense of the injury.

Such laws present a multitude of problems for facilities in terms of keeping people safe from harm while they are in a nursing home or rehab center. Mattresses are placed on the floor or beds are put in the lowest position so that they are no more than a foot from the floor. Patients who are at risk for falling need to be monitored closely at all times at great cost to the facility.

At Pleasantville, I was replaced by a lesser experienced nurse practitioner because it tried to protect a patient from harm. A nurse called me in the early morning hours and said that she found Mr. Larson with his head stuck in the side rail of his bed and he was non-responsive. Since the home is fairly close by, I got dressed and went over to see the patient. Mr. Larson, indeed, was non-responsive. His skin was dry, hot and it made a perfect tent when I held it between thumb and index finger then released it. I wrote in the chart what had occurred and sent the patient to the emergency room by ambulance.

The next day as I arrived at Pleasantville, I was greeted at the front door by the administrator. In his hand he held my notes from Mr. Larson's chart. He steered me into a nearby conference room. "Mrs. Michael, I have your notes on Mr. Larson from yesterday. I believe you have made some grave errors that need to be corrected immediately." He said as he handed them over to me. I read them and found no grave error as he had put it.

"I think it's pretty accurate. The patient was non-responsive, had many signs of dehydration and according to the nurse was found with his head was stuck in the side rails." I handed the papers back as I got up to leave.

"Sit there! You are not going anywhere yet!" he said sternly. He took out his cell phone and called Dr. Big Guy, who is, by the way, the medical director of the facility. He told him that I refused to change my entry in the patient's chart, then he handed me the phone. When I put it to my ear I heard Dr. Big Guy.

"What the hell do you think you are doing? What is wrong with you?" he demanded to know. "Change that charting now before you bring the state down on them! Do you understand me?"

Shocked and awed by his manner I replied, "Yes Sir! I hear you loud and clear." I rewrote my note to read as follows "patient found by nurse to have mental status changes. He was transported to hospital for evaluation and fluid replacement therapy." Mr. Larson never returned to the facility and later died of his many ailments.

Making laws that say certain things are never permitted to happen in these facilities absolutely changes nothing for the individuals who are entrusted to their care. The law only served to change the wording and did nothing to prevent these occurrences. It was purely an exchange of words, not a solution to the problems that plague long term care facilities. Our sick and elderly are confined to facilities for care they really don't receive. To be clear, however, is it not written that you can't say dehydration, bowel impaction or head stuck between side rail and bed. It is merely understood throughout the industry that you are never to say these things. If they are never documented, they never occurred is the philosophy. Meaning, what you say and saying what you mean is never tolerated in any nursing, rehab, hospital or mental health facility.

I, as a healthcare provider, can't insure that a patient gets water regularly by writing an order. I can't say "Push fluids with each meal" because this is a nursing order and not a medical one. I can however, write that the patient should receive 250cc of water each time he is given medication and this is acceptable. If the patient takes meds three times a day I can maybe count on him receiving three glasses of water. I have written this on almost every chart of every patient. Is it ever done? I couldn't say for sure. Many patients suffer from adult onset failure to thrive. Each patient gets a thimble full of water with their meds. If the medication nurse has to give any more, it would require her to go back and forth to fill the water receptacle on the med cart. She has to pass meds to a whole floor of patients which can be eighty people. Meds are given three times a day or more in an eight or twelve hour shift. If the patient can swallow the meds with a thimble full of water then that is all they are given.

After several months, I wondered if Leda had any of the same problems at Pleasantville. I wondered if it was just yours truly who couldn't go with the flow and not worry about such details. I needed to know if I was the only one who wondered if the patients were getting enough water, the meds I ordered or getting fed. Did staff get them in and out of bed when needed? I was at my desk in the office one afternoon doing my paper work. It was an alcove in the hallway just outside Dr. Big Guy's office. I overheard him talking to Leda. I didn't want to eavesdrop but it was hard not to when their voices were so loud. Leda complained to him about the home and how orders were not done for the most basic care. "Oh, stop it, will you? Let's just go have a drink somewhere you will be fine." He said to her and they were off. I saw her bring all of her charting from Pleasantville to the office. She wrote her notes there. She wrote the same thing over and over on each sheet for each different patient while Dr. Big Guy checked them and said, "Good Job! Good job!"

Such practices were illegal. Doctoring up records is also morally wrong. I felt dismayed and overwhelmed. I tried to talk to Dr. Big Guy. I told him I didn't like to lie just to keep my job. "Do not be stupid!" He says. "There is nothing illegal about changing you own notes. This goes on every day, everywhere in the industry. We have to keep ahead of those bastard lawyers so we don't get sued." I made my retreat from his office while thinking 'evil happens when good men do nothing'.

There are all kinds of loopholes in the law. I hoped retirement would bring me some peace of mind. I could deal with all kinds of sickness and devastation. There wasn't much I hadn't seen of terrible human suffering over the last fifty years in the care of others. I couldn't seem to abide by the politics. Dealing with illness was so much easier. I am pleased when things go well; the patient gets better and returns to life in the community. I can't get over social injustices that exist for those who are at the mercy of others who care for them. Writing brings some relief from the guilt I suffer when I see these things going on around me I can't control. There is power behind words when people read them and take action to defend the ones they love who cannot defend themselves.

When I listened to the homily in church on Sunday morning, the priest said that none of us are here by accident. We all have a role to play. We are links in a chain that is a vast network of humanity.

We are bound to each other and need to find our place and what it is we are to do. We may never know the answer until we meet our Maker. All we can do in the meantime is know this and try 'to love one another as God has loved us'.

Chapter 13

Be Good To Your Children, They Choose Your Nursing Home

A plaque that hangs outside my condo door says "be good to your children, they pick your nursing home". I have had this piece of art since the nineties after my first long battle with breast cancer. No truer words were ever spoken in the whole of the English language as far as I am concerned. My parents were healthy people and did not require any type of nursing home or long term care facility. My mother was only in a rehab center briefly after she sustained a fractured hip. It was the worst four weeks of my life. She had become so disoriented and had no idea where she was or what had happened to her. While my nurse's brain knew that it is common in the elderly, it was very hard to see and accept. Her mind began to clear almost immediately upon arriving back at her farm. She recovered quickly in her own surroundings. She was able to return to her normal activities of daily living. We were fortunate to have had her in a fairly nice rehab. But even it lacked the kind of caring people that should have been there to make her feel safe and comfortable.

A friend of mine, who happens to be a physician, had his mother in a facility in the south. He spent her entire fortune getting her the best care her money could buy. She lived a good life and died at the age of ninety-five. Good care in a facility is possible if you have an enormous amount of the green stuff. My friend and his mother had the money and he was the kind of son who was more than glad to spend it all on her. "It was, after all, her money." He once told me. Some children are not so willing to part with the family fortune so that mom or dad can live well in their final years. Those who are not wealthy may end up in a public aid facility. They are even worse than the ones I dealt with every day. They rely entirely on public funds for their day to day running. Most hire indigent people to take care of the indigent. They are managed by those who got the job because they were owed something from a local politician.

My African American friends have the right idea. Most of them care for their elder or special needs family members at home. My friend, Zev, was one of these most caring sons. One day I looked up and saw him coming toward me down the hall in my office. He had big tears running down his face. He said "Mary, my mama has passed. I miss her so much! What shall I do without her?" I tried my best to comfort and console him. His mother had a wonderful life although her parents had been born into slavery just before the civil war ended. The family's life had been hard but Ulla May had been educated and brought up well. She had only one child whom she loved and adored. Zev took very good care of her and her sister in their golden years. She died at the age of ninety-eight and her sister, who was older, was still living and well in her own home in the south. When a child is raised with love and respect they will love and respect others. Although my friend was lost without his dear mother, I think he could console himself with the fact that he cared for her and gave her a very comfortable life. She never saw the inside of a nursing facility.

Most people are unaware of the conditions that exist in at least ninety percent of nursing homes. Some feel they have no choice but to use them. Research shows that elderly and others, who are unable to care for themselves for whatever reason, fare much better at home in their own surroundings. Sometimes a parent raises many children, but sometimes it is difficult for these children to take care of one parent. In some states, a child can actually receive payment for care of a loved one at home. These programs, of course, are not widely publicized but they are available for those who care to seek them out.

John was one of my patients who had been confined to a wheelchair. He was a quadriplegic who is in his early forties and has been disabled since a young man due to an auto accident. He can move his arms a little and he can operate a motorized wheelchair. He had a care giver for about sixteen hours a day. The other eight hours, he was put to bed and was alone in his home. He had a van with a lift and he is able to get out and about with the help of his care giver who accompanies him to the doctor, shopping and social events. He had a special phone that responds to the sound of his voice so he can call almost anywhere or call for help. The cost to the state Medicare/Medicaid was about one fourth of the cost for care in a facility. I was totally baffled when I had to go to court and testify on his behalf so he could remain in his own home with his care giver as he is permanently disabled with no chance of recovery. I had to do this several times. I didn't mind but it seemed such a waste of time and money to tie up the courts with this kind of case. It had cost me much money as well. During my last appearance on his behalf, I attempted to point out this fact to the court and the judge. "Please answer the questions and sign the forms before you, Mrs. Michael. The court is not interested in, nor asking for your personal opinion or advice regarding this case. Please reframe from giving it," the judge said. I sat in that hearing very frustrated. I was called to these hearings for John every six months. It was worth it to me to lose a half day's pay. Dr. Big Guy saw no reason for it, so he refused to pay when I had to testify. I liked seeing the smile on John's face when we won approval for him to remain at home. I liked seeing him live his life to the fullest. I wondered who would fight for John, the handsome quadriplegic after I retired. Mother Theresa always had the right idea. She took care of all those indigent people washing them, feeding them, giving them medication but most of all she and her fellow nuns gave them dignity and comfort in their time of need. If I have done nothing else in my life time, this, I hope I have done.

Every individual should think of what may lay ahead for them one day. Perhaps, because I worked in the field every day, I tended to think about the future. Letting family and loved ones know how you wish to be cared for when the time comes is essential. Letting them know your wishes will save them, as well as yourself, a lot of heartache and uncertainty when faced with debilitating illness. When misfortune strikes, your mind may not be clear enough for you to articulate your needs. I have warned my children repeatedly in written and spoken word; do not spend money on nursing homes and fancy care for me. If I become too ill and too weak to care for myself, I have asked them to just leave me alone. Shut the condo door, lock it then come back in a few weeks when it is all over. They think my plan morbid and cruel. I think dying in your own home, on your own terms, a blessing. I want to be carried home while I am surrounded by my books, photos of my family and loved ones with the wonderful classical music of my life playing softly. I can't think of a better way to go.

While leaving the post office one day, I met an old friend. She waved and smiled greeting me in the sun light of a cold December afternoon. "Mary! I'm so glad to see you. Are you still practicing?" she asked.

"Janet, it's great to see you too. Yes, I am still in practice." I replied. "You know you can't take the nurse out of nursing." Running into that old friend gave me a warm feeling and brought back good memories of days gone by.

"You know, I was wondering if you would be willing to take on the care of my parents?" she asked. "My father is now ninety-two and it is hard to get him out of the house when he needs to see his doctor who thinks he should be in a facility. You know I don't want him going there or to the hospital anymore. They do nothing for him there anyway. I can do almost everything for him at home but with your help, we could have everything he needs. Please come to my parent's house and meet them to see if you want to take them on." I agreed to meet with them at her parent's house the very next day. I was working independently, in my own office and consulting with my collaborative physician when the situation called for it. I ran my own office for ten years. I loved it although it was very hard to get paid. I was constantly battling with insurance companies for payment. I would have done it for the rest of my life if I had been able to make a decent living without work elsewhere to supplement my income.

Janet's parents lived in a modest house on a quiet street in the suburbs. I was impressed with how well her mother handled her ailing father. She was just as old as he at the time. She was small very thin but she seemed to possess the strength of a team of horses. "I can't get my dad out of the house anymore. I don't want him in a home either. I want both of my parents to be able to live in their own home and die here too." Janet said with hope in her big blue eyes.

"Ok, Janet, I guess I'm up for a challenge." I replied. I got on well with her parents. I was looking forward to caring for them both. I consulted with their family physician who agreed with my plan of care. If Mr. Stone required any extra ordinary equipment or care, we would provide it. Janet was also a nurse so we were able to meet any need that arose. We even gave him IV fluids and meds at home. We placed his hospital bed in the middle of the living room so he would be in the heart of the home and all activities that went on there with their many children and grandchildren.

Over the next few months we fed Mr. Stone whatever he wanted to eat and he ate pretty well mostly very healthy foods. Janet, her mother, her brothers and sisters took turns bathing, turning and get him out of bed. He was moved every two hours during the day and at night it was every four hours. He was comfortable, free from pain and his skin never broke down. He had an untreatable cancer somewhere in the GI tract. Due to his age and congestive heart failure no treatment was possible for him.

Mr. Stone died on a sunny Sunday morning in April of the following spring. He was in his hospital bed in the middle of the living room. In attendance were his priest from the local church, his children, grandchildren and great grandchildren. We encircled his bed holding hands praying and singing him into the next life while he fell asleep in Christ. I have never attended a more peaceful death of a patient in my entire career as a nurse or nurse practitioner.

I continued to care for Mrs. Stone. She was able to see me in my office. When she began to fail, I went to her home. She didn't want hospitalization or any fancy medications. She suffered from dementia, from small vessel disease of the brain. I gave her meds to build her appetite as it is one of the main problems with dementia patients. They lose their taste for food. When the time came, she also went to join her husband much the same way.

Tending to patients in this manner was not as easy as I may be making it sound and that was true in the case of the Stones. There was opposition from the medical community who claimed that the couple should have been made to go into a nursing home. Mr. Stone should have been evaluated in the hospital and treatment attempted for his cancer which had spread by the time I started to care for him. Going up against the powerful medical community wasn't easy but I was able to do it because I had the support of the family doctor and the entire Stone family. The cost of their care to the insurance companies and Medicare was a fraction of what it would have been had they gone to hospital or nursing facility.

The Stones had the advantage of a loving family who gave of themselves freely to their beloved parents. All family members are not capable of giving care or have the time to do it. If a nursing facility is inevitable for a parent or loved one, there are things that can be done to make the decision of where placement should be easier. There are a few simple rules to follow when choosing a home in order to get the best one possible at reasonable cost. It is not a secret formula that no one else has, but these rules are seldom discussed with patients and their families because, as professionals, we can't favor one place over another. It is illegal and unethical to do so. While my list may be generic, it is very practical and easy to apply anywhere when looking for nursing and or rehab care.

The list of my pointers on selecting a nursing facility was both a convenience and a curse for the wife of one of my patients. When she had to choose a rehab center for her husband, I gave her the list of points I had devised that needed to be covered when conducting the search for just the right facility. I had created a brochure on how to find the best home for a loved one. "Alright Carol, study this carefully and make sure you cover every one of these points when you meet with the home for a tour. If they can't give you a good answer to any of these inquiries put a red circle around each one. Take a fresh copy for each place you visit and write the name of in on the brochure," I told her. Carol, a very intelligent woman who happened to be very tall and attractive with long silver gray hair, dressed smartly as well.

Late one night I received a call from her, "Mary, I'm sorry to be calling you so late but I must talk to you about the nursing home search. Your list has been both a help and a hindrance in this process."

"Why Carol? What has happened, please tell me?" I asked her anxiously. After all I had worked very hard on compiling it and it was the first time I had given it to anyone to use.

"Well, when I went to the first facility and I took out my list the administrator in charge of admissions and tours eyed me suspiciously. When we were done she told me that there were no beds available but she had told me over the phone that they always had accommodations. I was puzzled but I left without questioning her," she told me.

"But tell me how did that place fare against my check list?" I asked.

"Not too good. I had at least five things red circled so that's why I didn't bother to ask why suddenly there were no beds available," she replied.

"Ok so go on and tell me about the others," I inquired anxiously.

"When I arrived at the next home and they were expecting me, when the person that greeted me saw me take out my list, her friendly face dropped. She told me she was sorry but she was unable to give me a tour that day. She asked me to call back in a week if I still wanted to see the facility." Carol went on. "I can't wait until next week my husband will be discharged in a few days."

"Were you able to get to any other places yet?" I asked.

"Yes, I went to one other place and it checked out pretty good, only one red mark. It was because open visiting required a phone call prior to arriving. But the scary thing was that when we were done the administrator, Mr. Hammond, came in and asked me if I was a reporter conducting a secret investigation for a TV news program! Can you imagine that?" Carol said in dismay.

"I believe I can but at least the place sounds promising! I want you to remember, Carol, that you are perfectly within your rights to ask these things of any home you visit." I replied.

"Well that is just what the man told me but he just wanted to be certain I wasn't a reporter with a hidden camera. I think I will probably go with this place since they seemed so open." Carol replied and I breathed a sigh of relief. She was much younger than her husband Dan. She had to work to support them because their insurance had run out. They were now using their savings to pay for the facility and they had no large fortune.

The first rule in my pamphlet stated that when getting out of the car at the facility, take a deep breathe. If you can smell the place, leave immediately! Do not even go inside. It is the first clue as to how well a facility is run and staffed. If it smells after you get inside, leave. It won't get any better. Be prepared to spend a lot of time visiting homes. Keep the gas tank full as you may have to travel quite a distance to find a good place.

After locating a home that doesn't smell, ask how many registered nurses, Licensed Practical nurses, and nurse's aides per shift are staffed on the unit your loved one will be on. At least one RN, one LPN and three aides for every thirty patients is a good number for the first two eight hour shifts. For the night shift there may be just one RN covering a whole floor but one LPN and two aides would be adequate staffing. Ask how often linens are changed and how many times in a twenty-four hour period fresh drinking water is delivered. Be sure to ask if food can be brought in to patients as long as it meets the requirements of the person's diet restrictions. Most places will have extra help at meal times for those who need help eating or need to be fed. Make sure to inquire about open visiting hours. Most places will have them with few limitations. If the facility does not have them leave because they may be trying to hide something, such as lack of staff on off shifts.

After a loved one is admitted to a facility, go there all the time, show up on every shift. The more visible you are the more likely it is your family member will receive the care they require. Take these opportunities to assess the staff and how they work. Learn all the names of the staff caring for your loved one. Keep a journal and write them down if you have difficulty remembering names. But do it as discretely as possible. Note takers are always viewed as trouble makers by staff. Make an effort to get to know the staff and be friendly with them. It never hurts to bring them a treat once in a while. Make them feel that you are partners with them in the care of your loved one. Ask all your friends and family members to assist in these tasks. The more visitors a patient gets the more attention from staff they receive. It helps relieve some of the burden on one particular family member if all participate in the loved ones care.

Cleanliness is always a problem in most facilities. If your loved one or his/her surroundings are unclean, ask for linens and cleaning utensils and start cleaning. This will bring the staff to your loved one's room to see what you are doing. It will also alert the staff member in charge. In future, they will make certain that your loved one receives the proper care and the room is maintained in the cleanliest fashion. The reason for such attention is that some homes have had judgments leveled against them in a court of law making them liable to pay for care that was provided by family or other outside help when they weren't able to demonstrate that they had performed these duties. It is a common occurrence. The state and other insurance companies may deny payment to the home.

One man, I recall, kept meticulous records of the care he provided his wife while she was in a nursing home. He changed her dressing and did her bath, turned and positioned her. He wrote down dates and times and exactly what he had done. The staff at the home was more than glad to allow him to give care. When he demanded payment for his services they refused. So he took them to court. Since they could produce no such documentation of wound care, turning, feeding and bathing, the judge ordered the home to pay the husband for every day that his wife was there convalescing.

Making friends with the staff is very important in your loved ones care. Bring them a little cake or cookies and make them feel that you are on their side in the care of the patient. Make sure family and friends can go there at meal times in order to insure that mom or dad is eating properly. Malnutrition is a common problem of the elderly and infirmed. It is considered a seminal event and is never supposed to occur so it is never to be discussed or written down. Adult failure to thrive is what will be written which implies that your loved one is just not eating and ready to die. It will never be written that the food was so bad that your mom or dad couldn't eat it or no staff was available for feeding patients.

The banana incident is an event I recall even to this today. A young thirty-eight year old HIV/AIDS patient was quite ill when he was placed in one of my many nursing facilities. He had wasted down to just skin over bones. He had some rather large infected open wounds that required IV antibiotic therapy and meticulous wound care. Nutrition was of the utmost importance to this individual.

In one of my journals, I had read an article about nutrition in the treatment of HIV/AIDS patients. A research study had shown a correlation between eating a banana every day and the lowering of the viral load in these patients. Although more research is needed and the direct connection was not clear, it seemed to me a good thing to try for this man. So I ordered that the patient get a banana on his breakfast tray every day, a seemingly simple and benign request. I had no idea it would start a whole industry wide incident that took on a life of its own!

When I arrived at the home the very next day I was greeted by the administrator and the director of food services. They both approached me as I entered the front door. The administrator was scowling as the director of food services held up my order in a fisted hand yelling "This aint gonna happen! I gotta order a ho crate ah them bananas fo you ta give one ta that patient every day."

"So is there a problem in doing this?" I asked

"Yeah they is. What I gwana do with a ho bunch ah those things? They gonna rot bafo he can eat em!" I was still taken back by the looks on their faces as we stood in the middle of the lobby discussing my banana order.

"Well since a banana is such a good source of nutrition, why don't you give them to other patients who might enjoy them and the benefits they bring? I agree that food should not be left to spoil," I replied looking from one to another and wondering why they didn't seem able to follow this logic.

"This won't be easy." The administrator had finally found her voice "It will be a big expense to the home. They will have to be special ordered."

"Bananas?" I said in a high voice.

"I don't think you understand how food service works in an institution like this," replied the administrator. "All the food that comes in is prepackaged canned or frozen we don't get anything that is not already cooked and ready to serve after heating it up. We don't have storage for fresh items or anyone to prepare them. If it is not in a box, bag or can the patients don't get it." I was standing there with my mouth open.

The patient had no family members who were willing or able to bring in bananas for him. I was forbidden to purchase them for him. He received one banana the whole six weeks he was there for care. The banana incident became big news throughout the nursing home industry and is still talked about to this day.

Reviewing the medication list for your loved one should be done periodically. You have a right to know what meds he or she is receiving. If the patient is on meds to control adverse behavior make sure the legal guardian, power of attorney for health care or the patient has signed a permit to be given them. The physician or health care provider who ordered it should also sign the form. Over medicating people in facilities happens quickly and easily. It is also considered a seminal event, never supposed to happen and never documented. Monitor your loved one for signs of an over medicated state. If he or she appears too somnolent or too sleepy and not responding to you when you visit, ask that the meds be held until your loved one returns to their normal state of alertness.

The main goal of health care is supposed to be the patient's return to the highest level of functioning that they can attain. The goal should always be to return the patient to their home, community and their normal activities of daily living whenever possible.

An elderly gentleman in one of my homes wanted to return home to his own apartment. He had been receiving some type of treatments for cancer that left him very weak but his mind was clear. One day he was transported by ambulance to the big university hospital to see a specialist. When the appointment was over he insisted that the ambulance driver return him to his apartment instead of the nursing home. Since he was alert and oriented the driver had no choice but to fulfill his wishes. He had been transported by a private ambulance company which meant that he was paying for it. When Dr. Big Guy found out this had happened he was very upset but could do nothing to return the patient to the home. I was never able to find out what happened to him after that but I hope he enjoyed being in his own surroundings. If he died, I hope it was there in his own home on his own terms.

Chapter 14

The Trial

Staying focused after resigning and announcing my retirement provled to be very difficult. Days seemed to get longer even though the end of summer was approaching. I had received a jury summons. I always felt it my duty to comply with these things if at all possible. I had, once again, become very tired and sleep deprived from being on call day and night. I took my summons to work and arranged to take the day off to go down to the big city and sit in the court room all day. I had a good book I wanted to read anyway. I never understand why people always want to get out of Jury duty because many are called but few are chosen. It is the perfect way to get a day off if you are a person like me who works every day of the week and then some that don't even exist. I enjoyed going to the big city, watching people and having lunch at a nice restaurant or café. So with good book in hand and the promise of a relaxing bright sunny day next morning, I headed for bed when my phone rang.

"Mary How are you? It's me Ann Marie. I want to know if you can come with me to the ball game tomorrow evening." She asked. She knew I loved our major league team on the big city's south side. She and her husband have season tickets with good seats right behind home plate. I loved going with her and eating a hot dog in the large open air stadium with all the fans screaming. The last time she took me along with her cousin and another lifelong friend of ours it was seventies night. We dressed up in afro wigs with big peace sign necklaces hanging from our necks, bell bottoms and big sun glasses. We danced in the stands to seventies hits and got ourselves on TV! My two daughters who happened to be watching the game that night were shocked and mortified to see their mother on TV. "Mother I hope no one recognized you. But I knew it was you in that silly costume!" My daughter scolded me the next day.

"Oh Ann Marie, you know I love going to the ball games with you. It will be the perfect end to a perfect day. I got a jury summons and will be down town anyway. When they let me go I'll just hang around down there and then meet you at the ball park. I couldn't ask for more! I get to sit in an air conditioned court room reading a good book. I'll take myself out to lunch, then go shopping and end the day watching my favorite team win a ball game along with some of my favorite people. Life is good Ann Marie, life is very good." I guess you know by now that it doesn't take much to make me happy. A good book, a day at the ball game, a little shopping and I feel as if I have died and gone to heaven! Simple pleasures for the simple minded.

After swinging the big town car onto the express way, I looked at my court summons. I realized that it was for the county court house on the west side of the city and not the big one down town. It was better because it was closer to the ball park. I didn't like going to the west side of the city as it is rather a dangerous place to visit, but the areas around the courts are very secure. I parked the car in a multi-level garage across the street from the large court house and took the crossway with everyone else. Dr. Big Guy wasn't happy that morning. He didn't want me to take more than a day off at a time. He never got over the fact that I had six days off in January when I fell and broke my arm. I assured him that nurses and doctors are rarely picked to be members of a jury. Due to the nature of our work, most attorneys feel we make bad jurors.

When I checked in at the desk I was surprised to see so few people. Usually there would be several hundred potential jurors summoned at once. As I looked about me, I saw a number I was certain didn't even equal one hundred. The waiting room was practically empty. We all sat and listened to jury instructions on a TV monitor over our heads that lasted about a half hour, then we went for coffee. I found a comfortable chair and proceeded to become very engrossed in my new best selling novel entitled "The Help".

I didn't realize so much time had passed until a clerk came to announce lunch time. She told us we were not allowed to leave the building. We were given a voucher for lunch in the court house cafeteria. I mourned my dreams of a nice lunch at a fancy dining place. I had to settle for a hamburger and a salad. We were given only forty minutes and then we were expected to go back to the waiting room and check in with the clerk again. At one in the afternoon the first pool of jurors was called into the court room. I breathed a sigh of relief when I was not among them. Twenty minutes later another group was called. I was almost sure I didn't hear my name called. To be certain, I went up to the clerk and asked if she had called me. She snapped at me for not responding when my name was called. She handed me a pass for court room forty-five and told me to hurry there before she called a bailiff to take me.

The room was very small and jammed packed with potential jurors and lawyers. I told myself just to sit tight, I would be soon excused and out of there in no time. I was only mildly worried when the judge took the stand and gave the toughest speech to jurors I had ever heard. "Ladies and gentleman," she began, "thank you for coming today. You have been summoned here as a potential juror in the trial of a young man accused of murder." When she said that I knew I wouldn't be on this jury. I certainly didn't believe in the death penalty! Then she continued "If you think you are too good or too important to be here, you would do well to think again. None of you are that important. If you think your job is too valuable to society for you to be here, trust me, it is not. If you think because this is a murder case and you do not believe in the death penalty, you will be excused, you won't. This is not a death penalty case. You will only be excused if being here causes you or a family member undue hardship or if you or a family member or anyone you know is connected to this case." When she made that last statement many hands began to shoot up into the air. She raised hers saying "No! Not now, I will ask the questions and I will decide if you stay or go. So sit back ladies and gentlemen as this is going to take quite some time to complete. I will interview each and every one of you and the attorneys for both the defense and the state will also have a chance to ask you questions. At this point we will take a short break. You will be able to make the necessary phone calls you need. You may use the bathrooms that are located in the adjoining room. There will also be some refreshments for you there as well. We will see you back here in court in twenty minutes."

Stunned and a little dazed, I stumble from the court room. After the women's bathroom, I called Ann Marie. I got her voice mail. I left her a message telling her I was going to be interviewed as a potential juror and I would call her back when I got out of court. The ball game was not scheduled to begin until seven that night so I thought I had plenty of time. I realized, with a little disappointment, that any shopping was clearly out for me. I decided to wait to call Dr. Big Guy because there was still a very good chance that I would never be selected as my profession had always gotten me off in the past.

The questioning of each person was intense and very in depth as well as very personal. There must have been fifty of us squeezed into the benches in that court room. I was sure the judge would never get to me. When I tried to read my book I found that I couldn't concentrate on it due to the proceedings going on around me. I started listening carefully to the questioning and found it intriguing to say the least. I heard my name being called after four hours in that court room of listening to others answer these very intrusive questions from the judge. I got to my feet and swore to tell the truth and nothing but.

"Mrs. Michael please state your full name and any other names you have used in your life, your age, date of birth and the approximate area in which you live" ordered the judge. She began to ask questions about my original name of Maria Evelina Veronica Rosario. I had to explain the whole story to her of how I ended up with the name I used now. I had to explain where I was born, who I had married and divorced. I had to answer all questions about my two daughters, where they went to school, what jobs they had, how many kids they had and to whom they were married. This judge was getting to know me better than some of my most intimate life long friends knew me. I was sure she was going to excuse me when I answered her next question. "Now Mrs. Michael tell me and the court what it is you do for a living."

"I'm a nurse practitioner in private practice with a physician in the south west suburbs of the city." Of course after that I was obligated to explain what a nurse practitioner was and what my profession entailed. She asked many questions about my practice. I was surprised she was so interested. "Very well, now Mrs. Michael, please look at the defendant in this case, tell me and the courts if you have ever seen this gentleman before, know him or anything about him or this case." She asked.

When I looked into the eyes of the young man going on trial for murder, I think it was the first time I had wished that it was someone that I knew. I had cared for many young black men like him in my long career but, unfortunately, he wasn't one of them. "No ma'am I do not know the gentlemen." I replied.

"Mrs. Michael have you ever been convicted of a crime?"

"No ma'am."

"Have you ever been the victim of a crime?"

"Yes Ma'am, I have."

"Please explain to the court the circumstances of the crime or crimes of which you were a victim."

"Well I had my car stolen from in front of my home in 1978 when I lived in the big city. Then in 1991 I had my purse stole out of the frontseat of my car while I was at a gas station pumping gas and later that same year I had another car stolen from the street in front of my home."

"Do you feel that being a victim of these crimes will influence you in any way should you be selected to serve on this jury?" she asked.

Here I saw my chance to lie through my teeth and tell her yes! But I'm a bad liar and I just couldn't do it just to get out of my civic duty as a tax paying voter in this county. "No ma'am it will not." I answered her.

"Tell me what you know about weapons Mrs. Michael, have you ever seen one, fired one or do you own one?"

"Yes ma'am I have been schooled in the use and handling of fire arms in the past when I was in the US Army Reserves. I fired an M-16 and a 45 hand gun. It was required for a commissioned officer. I do not own a fire arm or have access to one since leaving the army more than twenty years ago." My God how much longer was I going to have to stand there so exposed?

"Mrs. Michael would you happen to be acquainted with any of the attorneys in the court room here today?" she asked.

"No ma'am, I am not." I replied.

"Do you happen to know any attorneys, Mrs. Michael?"

"Yes ma'am, I know quite a few."

"Who might they be and what is your relationship with them?"

"Excuse me? All of Them?"

"Yes Mrs. Michael, all of them."

"Well, there is Mr. Zachery, my own personal attorney and my friend Mr. Stanly Zewicki's son by the same name. I also know Mr. Foley another friend and….." I continued naming names both friends and other lawyers I had known throughout my years working in politics. "I also have several attorneys, patients of mine whom I can't name due to the privacy act."

"Will knowing these attorneys have any effect on your judgment should you be selected today as a juror in this case?" She asked. There was another chance for me to answer in the affirmative and maybe get myself off from jury duty. She hadn't excused anyone yet, not even the man who said he was an attorney or the man who said he had just been on a jury for another murder trial. He stated that he sure wasn't keen on the idea of going through another in less than a year.

"No ma'am it will not." I heard myself say. After four grueling hours we were given a break. I took the time to check my cell and saw that my friend had called me back. I took a bottle of water and a piece of fruit from the snack room and called her back.

"Annie, I'm still here and we have been grilled like hamburgers by this judge! My Lord is she tough. I didn't know they were allowed to ask so many personal questions. It isn't looking good for me. I was sure she wouldn't pick me but she has interrogated us all. They are all in a meeting now, she and the defense and prosecution lawyers, to go over our profiles and selected the ones they want. I sure hope it won't be me. I don't want to be on a murder trial".

"I don't know why you are down there anyway! Why didn't you just ask Clark to get you out of it?" she asked. She is married to my attorney. She must know me by now and know that I wouldn't have done it. I knew it was my civic duty to be there. While I wasn't happy about it, I knew if I were involved in some type of litigation I would expect others to step up to the plate and do jury duty.

"It is so late now Annie and they are about to call us back in. I'll call you when I'm in my car on my way to the ball park. I have to hang up now and turn my cell off again." I quickly hung up as a tall bailiff walked toward me with a look of stern authority.

"Cell phone off ma'am and you must get back in the court room. The judge is about to reenter for the selection of jurors." He stared down at me. I pushed the off button and followed him back into the court room.

I was squeezed in once again in the last row of benches on the very end. We all came to our feet when the judge returned to the bench and called the court to order. There was another twenty minute side bar conference among the lawyers and the judge. Then she began to call names asking each of them to stand. As the rest of us sat and listened. "The ladies and Gentlemen who are now standing are excused at this time. Thank you for your time and please leave quietly from the side door." she then asked the gentleman to stand that had said he had served on a jury for a murder case within the last year. "You are an outstanding citizen, sir. You have served the court of this county well. I shall not keep you here any longer imposing on your generosity of service. Thank you for your time. You are free to go." The man breathed a deep sigh of relief as his face took on a lighter expression. He departed the room.

One by one the judge called the names of those who would be serving on the jury. As each person stood there she questioned them intently as to whether they were committed to serve and able to do the whole trial which she said she was sure would last only for a week. I was almost off the hook as I kept track of how many people she had called. I had counted fourteen when I heard her say will Mrs. Mary

Michael please stand. Giving a slight gasp, I got to my feet. I was asked all of the same questions as the others. She then proceeded to name all of us again giving us numbers. I was number twelve and the last three people were the alternates.

My watch said seven-thirty when I was being escorted to my car by two large county sheriffs' police who were dressed in full protective gear carrying shot guns. "You know fellows if anyone were to shoot at us I would be the one to die here." I said trying a light approach as I looked up from one to the other on each side of me. I don't think they saw the humor in the situation.

The walk to the car felt like a death march because I still had to call Dr. Big Guy and let him know that I had been selected for the jury. I wouldn't be back to work for a week or be able to be on call. We were told we couldn't have our cell phones or talk to anyone during the trial. We were instructed to speak to no one regarding the case. We were told to come early to court and to be prepared to stay late. We would be locked into the court room until we were let out to go home. We would have no contact with anyone and we would be searched every day. We were warned that we were never to speak to anyone in or around the court. We were never to make eye contact with anyone in or out of court as this could cause a mistrial and they would have to start the process all over again.

"Hi Doctor its Mary."

"I know it is you. What do you want?" he yelled into his cell phone.

"I got selected to be on the jury for a murder case and I won't be at work for the next week and I'm not allowed to have a cell phone so I can't be on call." I replied and braced myself for the onslaught of his wrath.

"How in the hell do you get yourself into this kind of mess? Well, I don't envy you but I guess we will manage without you somehow. God knows we will have to soon enough." He replied.

"Thank you, sir, for your understanding." I said as I hung up and made my way to the ball park. The game was well under way when I finally arrived. The air was crisp and clear and the hot dogs were so good. The comfort and conciliation of my friends was most welcome. We had a wonderful time and of course our team, the home team, won the game.

Over the weekend Dr. Big Guy gave me all of the calls for all of the nursing homes because he thought it unfair to Leda that she should have my calls for the next week. As far as I could tell, she hardly ever took her own call for her homes. I had it most of the time with the exception of the time I broke my arm. Knowing that I wouldn't have any calls for a week made the task of juror seem a lot less. I got very little sleep over the weekend with my cell and home phone going off every ten minutes and sometimes they would ring simultaneously. Our answering service has a large staff of operators who take calls for many practices. I try to be patient with them because I know that they are only the messengers and have nothing to do with the nature of the calls.

On Monday morning I called service to let them know I wouldn't be on call all week due to being on a jury. I wasn't surprised to learn my office hadn't informed them. I gave the supervisor all the information of those who would take my calls. "I hope everything goes ok for you, Mary, we here at the service will be praying for you. You know we will miss you. We hate it when you're not on call because you're always so pleasant to us."

"Well, thank you Doris, I try to never take it out on you when I get some of these crazy calls. I really wanted some time off but this wasn't exactly what I had in mind." I said with a little giggle.

"I bet it wasn't! You take care of yourself down there ok?"

"Thank you Doris, I will." I turned off my cell phone and entered the building. I went through the metal detector and then I was searched by a female officer who nodded me through to the other side. I made my way up to court room number forty-five. I was greeted by a bailiff who confiscated my cell phone and escorted me into a side room off the court room where other jurors were waiting.

"Ladies and Gentlemen you will get your cellphones back at the end of the day. I will be with you all day. There are two rest rooms to your right. You are not allowed to leave this court under any circumstances. We will be serving you lunch here as well as other snacks and refreshments. The judge will make sure you get breaks as needed. No one else is allowed in this room. Remember when you are called into the court room you must not make eye contact with anyone other than the judge, attorneys, defendant and witnesses who are called to testify. Should you break this rule a mistrial may be called and the process will have to start over again. You must not fall asleep or otherwise be inattentive in court. You will listen to all of the instructions the judge gives you. Please help yourself to coffee and rolls and wait here until I come for you. Thank you," the bailiff said and left the room.

I was glad I brought my good book again because there was a lot of hurry up and then wait. The courts in this big city are so crowded with cases that it was difficult to find a room in which to try this young man. There was a long delay in getting started. The man on trial was in his thirties and sat stoically throughout the proceedings. It seemed to me none of the people involved in this case were what you would call model citizens. They appeared to be members of rival gangs. They had gotten into a dispute at a night club on the city's south side. The young man on trial was supposed to have shot and killed another young man at close range. Members of both gangs were present in the court room as well as family members of both victim and the accused. Their presence made the rule of not making eye contact with any of them very difficult as there were many out bursts of emotion on all sides.

The attorneys for the state seemed to be much better trained and prepared for the case than did these public defenders for the accused. I listened intently at every word. The first two hours went by very quickly.

When the noon hour approached the judged declared a recess. We were, once again, escorted out of the court room by our bailiff. Much to my surprise, the judge and everyone else in the court were asked to rise while the jury was being dismissed. The judge explained as we slowly stood up that it was proper court room procedure during a trial. I hadn't been aware of that rule before serving on that jury. There was hot food in tin foil trays waiting for us when we were back in the side room. Since I was used to serving a big family, I washed my hands and began filling plates with food and passed them around. The veggies I could recognize but the meat was a mystery. So it went that we had some type of mystery meat every day. The food was pretty awful.

At the end of that day and every day during the trial, all twelve of us and the three alternates were given back our cell phones. We were again surrounded by county sheriffs in full protective gear prior to being escorted right to our cars in the parking garage. We were instructed to drive straight home and not to talk to anyone who tried to stop us and engage us in conversation. I guess I should have felt safe with all these armed guards around but it only served to make me more uneasy very day.

All that week we had a lot of down time. We were always told that we could not discuss the case. Being crammed together in such close proximity in that little room, we began to talk to each other. We got to know one another in a way that strangers might when meeting on a vacation. I found my fellow jurors to be good honest people from all walks of life. There was John the warehouse manager and Liam the architect as well as a school teacher, an administrative assistant and a young man looking for work. We began to come together as a group. We cared about each other as if we were in some kind of life crisis.

When witnesses were called to the stand I listened intently to everyone's testimony. I came to realized that the people involved in the case were definitely rival gang members. They had gone to a club on the south side of the city for a night out where a dispute had occurred between the members. I understood the gentleman accused was allegedly carrying a gun and pulled it out and shot another man at point blank range killing him instantly. However, no weapon was found at the scene or on the accused when he was arrested a few blocks away from where the crime had allegedly occurred.

Some of those called to testify used language unfit for human ears! It was certainly not what you would expect in a court of law. Some of the witnesses were incarcerated already, clade in orange jump suits, hand cuffs and chains with hobbles on their ankles. When they were asked directly about the night in question, they refused to answer or just let out a long string of words I could not put down on paper. I didn't see the point in having them testify. I was really beginning to feel very confused. I realized that none of these folks would be anyone I would want to have lunch with any time soon. That went for the witnesses on both sides.

Every day of the trial we were moved around to different court rooms due to overcrowding. We ate that lunch of mystery meat day after day. There was still a lot of downtime so I managed to finish one book and start another as well as catch up on reading my periodicals. As we approached the fourth day of the trial I had to acknowledge the fact that the attorneys for the prosecution were mounting a better case each day. I was beginning to see the fate of this young man at the hands of public defenders. The prosecution was quick to offer objections and had hard hitting questions for all of the witnesses. Since there continued to be long periods of down time most days, we were not dismissed until after nine o'clock at night. I came home just as exhausted as if I had put in a full day at work. Although I wasn't on call I still had a hard time falling asleep knowing I had the fate of another human in my hands. If convicted he would spend the next twenty-five years in prison, a large portion of his youth. I wanted a little time off work but the respite I was looking for was not in that court room.

On the following Friday we finally got the case with many instructions from the judge on what was expected of us. I hadn't slept well all week because I still wasn't convinced beyond a reasonable doubt that the defendant shot and killed the victim. The two men confronted each other, there was an argument, shots were heard, and the defendant walked away, the victim fell to the ground and died. No one said for sure that they saw a gun in the defendant's hand. No gun was found on him when he was arrested a few blocks away. Witnesses said that they heard shots ring out and they all ran. Not one of them said that they saw a weapon on the defendant. While I understood that none of these characters involved in this case were model citizens and most of them probably belonged behind bars for the safety of the whole community, I just couldn't say the defendant was guilty. I'm a stickler for details due to the nature of my work. I know that the slightest change in a person's laboratory values can mean a serious problem. The whole of my day and the decisions I make regarding the health of another human being lies in the details of the case.

The type of logic I used in my everyday life is what I brought to the court room that day we got the case. We selected Liam as our jury Foreman. That process went well and very quickly. Liam read the judge's instructions to us again and also the charges against the defendant, and then we took a vote. It was eleven to one that he was guilty. I guess I need not tell you who couldn't pull the trigger. When I expressed my concerns to the other jurors, there were two more that stated that they had the same doubts. They said they were reluctant to bring it up as all the other jurors were convinced of his guilt. I was also concerned that testimony from other witnesses who were there that night was never heard. When I brought this point up, it was revealed that some of them had been shot and killed in other gun battles across the city.

"Mary, I want you to be sure of your decision so we will review the trial records of the witnesses who were closest to the victim that night." Liam offered. We spent the next two and a half hours reviewing notes. When the next votes were cast I was able to say without a reasonable doubt that the defendant was guilty as charged. We sent a note to the judged indicating that we had reached a verdict. Everyone in the court room came to their feet when we entered.

After Liam read the verdict the judge addressed each of us by name. We had to stand up and answer questions related to our vote of guilty. "Mrs. Michael, please stand and tell the court, when you found the defendant guilty as charged, did you come to your decision of your own free will?"

"Yes your honor, I did." I replied.

"Did anyone attempt to coerce or bribe you into this decision?" she asked.

"No ma'am they didn't." I answered. She continued to ask these questions of every juror. I felt relieved that I had gone through the process of coming to a guilty verdict by reviewing all the evidence in the case. After the verdict was read, a large commotion erupted in the court room among the members of the defendant's family. They were the ones always trying to get our attention and disrupt the court in order to get a mistrial called. They put on quite a show. All in all it was practically like any court trial you would see on TV but with a lot of down time.

Everyone stood again as we were escorted out of the court room and once again in the secured room behind it. We were told to wait there for the judge. After about an hour she came in to speak to us. She thanked us for our service and told us that we had done a good job. "You will not be called again for at least five years after all of the paper work from this trial is filed." She told us. "You are all free to go but you will be escorted to your cars so wait here for the sheriffs' police to take you to the garage." She then came to each of us individually shook hands and thanked us personally.

We were alone again in the room when nine of the jurors and the two alternates came to me and thanked me for making them review the evidence again. "I really wasn't all that sure, myself, and I was glad that we went over everything again. Now I can forget about this stuff and go on with my own life." I was relieved most of them didn't hold it against me that I had made them stay here longer to reach this decision. The armed guards came for us and we were escorted from the courts once more under heavy surveillance. Liam walked beside me and took my hand. A man with a Hispanic accent who had been on the jury with us came up behind us.

"Man I only live a few blocks from here I'm almost scared to walk home. I think I'm going to jog all the way."

"Go on I'm watching you." one of the armed offices said. We shook hands with him and watched him run down the street.

"Thank you again for today and this whole week. I've been on jury before and I've been a foreman but nothing like this. I'm glad you were here I don't think I could have done this without you." Liam said. When we approached my car, we were standing there with tears in our eyes. We hugged each other tightly with all those guards watching.

"It's really hard to let go." But we finally parted with the hope of meeting again. People can't be brought together like this without forming some sort of bond with each other as Liam and I had done. It was almost like the bond that I formed with most of my patients. It reminded me that I had to contact Dr. Big Guy and let him know that I was once again available for call.

"You done with all that business now!" he barked into the phone.

"Well we had a little trouble reaching a verdict but we finally did it." I replied.

"Did you find him guilty?" He asked "Yes sir, we did." I said, quietly.

"Now let me guess, there was one juror who could not commit to guilty and that is what took you so long. Am I right?" he asked.

"That is right sir." I answered reluctantly.

"Oh let me guess! That one juror was you. God you have to make such a big deal out of everything. I don't know how you can stand yourself." He said and hung up the phone. It wasn't five minutes later when my cell started to ring with a message every few minutes from the service. I was busy all night and all weekend taking calls. There was no time to unwind and reflect on the events of the past week. The bright side was that I wouldn't be called for another trial for a long time and I only had five more weeks to work with Dr. Big Guy.

Chapter 15

Go And Tell All People

It was a beautiful fall day as I was winding down to the finish line of my life long career and my days with Dr. Big Guy. He was still convinced that I would take a vacation and return in a month. Some of my friends believed it as well. Nettie, for one, kept saying that she knew I wouldn't retire. "You can't stay away from your work. I know you can't. It's one of the reasons you and Zev get on so well. You're two of a kind because he can't stop working either. You both have that intense type "A" personality."

I have had been planning my escape from full time work for what seems like an incredible amount of time, even before I went to work for Dr. Big Guy and those horrible substandard nursing facilities. Five years ago I had my own office. I was practicing on my own which is perfectly legal in this state. The much laid back and mild mannered Dr. Nelson was and still is my main collaborative physician. Back in the early days of my career I had been working hard with my organization to get the state to let Nurse Practitioners bill directly for services rendered to patients receiving public assistances. The reason I supported it was I believed it to be a good option for patients. I thought we would provide better care to those in need in an efficient and cost effective manner. Routine health care, care of minor illnesses and injuries, and preventative care are the domain of Nurse Practitioners. It freed up the mainstream health care system for the more acutely ill. I had run my own campaign with one of the largest third party payers in the state. I had gotten them to reimburse me for my services at a rate of eighty-five percent of what they would pay a physician for the same services. It was the same rate of reimbursement that the federal government gave us for Medicare patients. When we finally got the state to agree to reimburse us, it was at one hundred percent of the rate that the physicians were paid. We felt that we had achieved a great thing indeed.

Billing for services rendered to patients who receive state aid proved to be harder than any of us had anticipated. If you worked in a hospital or large clinic there would be a whole staff of people in billing. In a solo practice it was much more difficult. I found myself spending more time on the paper work than taking care of the patient. I discovered that I was unable to get paid from the state. Since I had worked on the bill, I couldn't just opt to pull out and stop accepting patients on public assistance.

I had little success in getting Dr. Nelson to understand what was occurring with reimbursement. I needed to do something in order to stay in practice. The other problem was that my health insurance had run out. I wasn't able to buy a policy on my own because of my many pre-existing conditions of cancer, diabetes and high blood pressure. There were some companies willing to insure me but at a premium and a deductible charge that Bill Gates would have had difficulty paying. I ended up moving my practice in with another physician. It was agreed that I would see all my patients as well as those of a departing physician from that practice. The practice would assume all responsibility for billing. I would have health insurance and my monthly salary as an employee of that practice. The compensation I was given was comfortable by most standards.

After a brief few months I began to see that the practice was poorly run and the care substandard. I tried but quickly learned that changing things would not be an option. Dazed and bewildered day in and day out while trying to see thirty-five patients a day while taking call almost every night, I began to lose focus. I wasn't spending quality time with my patients because there was none to spare. They were being herded in and out of the office like cattle. They were getting little or no real care. Then Dr. Big Guy started calling, asking me to come to work for him. "Look I have heard all about you from other physicians. I am busy and need your help in the office and with nursing homes." I received his calls every few days until I finally gave in and agreed to meet with him. Over dinner, he was very convincing that it would be of mutual benefit to join his practice. He made it sound as if my life would be a little easier to stay in practice a little longer as I was already retirement age when we met. I would be able to provide the kind of care that my patients had come to expect from me. Soon after I joined him, it became quite evident that I had jumped from the frying pan into the fire. The only thing that had changed was the location of my office. It was the same type of staff, poorly trained, rude and uncaring. My office hours were cut so I could spend more days in the nursing homes and my nights on call. I didn't see my final contract until after I had left the other practice. It was less pay for more work. I had been trapped into it by fast talking, charming Dr. Big Guy. It all happened some time ago but it felt as if a life time had passed.

Some months after, I notice that he became more subdued around the office. He confided in me that he had to curtail his activities of drinking and running around with young women late at night. It came about not because of his conscience or his wife's disapproval; it had been the doing of our suburb's finest men in blue. They had issued him a ticket for DWI. Such things are a matter of public record when it requires a court appearance. He didn't want that kind of publicity. An indiscretion such as a DWI is never good for the practice and may put ones license at risk. Over those last few weeks he asks almost daily if I have changed my mind about retirement. "No sir, I have not changed my mind. I really need to get my health back and take better care of myself if I'm going to be able to spend any quality time with my grandchildren." I told him.

"Well it's all your own doing you know. You could take more time off or ask me to take your calls for you oncein a while." He offered. I was well aware it would never happen. The few days that I had taken off were a major problem for him. He made it clear, in no indirect way, that he didn't like it when I took any sort of time off.

Determined to write my memoirs about life in the nursing homes and rehab centers, I knew there would be no turning back. Although I have not named names or places, I have burnt my bridges. I hoped to get the news out all over many towns, communities, and hopefully many states. I hoped to make people everywhere aware of the problems and injustices that are suffered by those who are confined to facilities. I believed then and now that only through knowledge and constant vigilance can we change things and protect those we love. We can't be sure what happens to those that have no one to advocate for them. Life is very hard for those without loved ones or family members. No matter how trying some may be, is better to have them than to be at the mercy of strangers.

Many may argue that those who end up on public care are dregs of society and deserve what they have gotten for what they have given in their time here on earth. Well I don't agree. We cannot sit in judgment of others as it is not our place. We cannot know what has occurred in any individual's life that might have brought them to the point in their lives when they are dependent on others for their care and survival. When someone is down and out they should not be further punished because they were not always a good person or a productive member of society. Kicking someone who is already down makes no sense to me. I don't think anyone of us can say that in his or her entire life they were always a good person. We are all generally good people, even the ones who seem to be all bad. After all, it is the life God gave them that we come to respect and celebrate. If we respect and honor another's life we are honoring God. I believe it to be the way we can pay homage to our Almighty Father. We can't see God or even know what He is thinking or feeling. We can see each other and know that weall need dignity and respect and proper care no matter how good or evil we may have been.

Physical, emotional and mental well being is at the heart of everyone's life. Without any one of these we are at the mercy of others, our government and the mighty health care system. People like Mariumamma and Sheila, Princess and Mrs. Martin were able to see the wound or the problem and treat it without holding the individual who has developed it in contempt for what he or she may have done in their lives to have ended up with the problem in first place.

There are many good physicians who really have the patient's best interest at heart. They are kind and patient people who have not had their souls crushed by the system and its red tape. They have not lost faith in dealing with a vocation that has turned into a business for profit instead of one of caring and kindness. Health care has come down to figuring out how much profit can be made and how the losses can be cut rather than how we can do the greatest good for the greatest number of people in the country. I know that Dr. Big was young and more of a business man that a humanist. I know that he was not all bad. I hoped that someday he will see the forest for the trees.

Chapter 16

The Farewell

The last day I worked came and went in the usual way. There was no fanfare and no band playing. I made a final visit to Whispering Pines before going to the office. It was a buzz with its usual hum of business when I arrived. The staff said little as the day came to a close. They all left expressing a few well wishes and then all was quiet. I was the last one to leave, as usual. Still there to the last minute clearing up things, refilling medications and returning phone calls. I had turned in my key so I wanted to make sure I had gathered all my belongings before I locked the door for the last time. I called the answering service and told them it was my last day; they were not to page me anymore after seven that evening. I felt tears coming to my eyes when the operators all took turns saying goodbye and telling how much they would miss me. "It is so much easier to talk to you than the others you never get mad at us or yell at us." They all said. I had always reminded myself that they were just the messengers and it was wrong to "shoot" at them even if the message was one I didn't want to hear.

While driving home I began to wonder, how does one say good bye and just stop working at a career that spanned almost fifty years? Was it going to be just that easy to leave and never look back? Would anyone remember who I was or that I cared for them with my whole heart and soul? I reckoned not. People are busy and life keeps on pulling you along just as it had pulled me along all those years as it did those who came before me. You live and you work and then you die. It occurred to me then that I was very fortunate because some never live to retire.

They may live and then die very quickly, never having had the opportunity of longevity or a long career.

When I arrived home I closed the condo door behind me and looked around. In the silence that consumed me, I wondered out loud, "What will I do here for the rest of my life?" The answer didn't come right away. I had a good dinner, watched some mindless TV shows and fell into a deep sleep. Then I woke listening for the phone and my pager. I was sure I heard them go off but I was mistaken. The reality that my last day at work had passed and there would be no more pages and no more phone calls began to sink in to my soul. Although I had been elated at the prospect of so much free time, the sadness of not being needed or wanted every minute of every day began to sink into my very being. I cried myself to sleep that night, something I hadn't done since my husband had walked out on me almost forty years ago.

In the early morning hours, I began reviewing everything that had taken place in the last few weeks. I knew I had closed the door on my entire working career in nursing homes. I had oriented a new nurse practitioner that would be taking my place. It was clear she wouldn't be putting herself out to do all the things I was doing for those people. I could see it in her eyes and read her quite well. Dr. Big Guy, I was sure, wouldn't raise any red flags either. Informing all my office patients had been a tedious task and one that I hoped never to repeat. Some of them would follow me to Dr. Nelson's office where I would still see patients one day a week. Others would stay with Dr. Big and yet more would seek other health care providers.

The sun was shining brightly as I sat in the bay window of the kitchen. I had coffee and a leisurely breakfast. I read a good book, and then I wandered from room to room. I started to notice how worn and dull looking everything had become. In the guest bedroom

I saw dull white walls and a faded out bed spread. "This doesn't look inviting at all!" I said out loud. Doing a little redecorating might be fun. The date for my retirement party had been set for November Twentieth. Overnight guests would be coming to town for it. I had about five weeks to do some overhauling. I began to make plans, starting with the guest room. The color was called "Hint of Mint" and I thought it worked quite well. I'm not a fan of loud or dark colors on the walls. Just two walls painted in that color was enough to brighten the room along with a new bedspread and pillows.

I was so pleased with the outcome that I decided to put the same color on two walls in the kitchen. It brought new life to the already bright space. I added a back splash that made it look new. The rainbow iridescent blue green glass tiles were a startlingly beautiful addition. After a good scrub the kitchen was done and it looked brand new. I added bright green, blue and yellow towels and accent pieces. I was beginning to enjoy decorating.

Tackling the living room and dining room was next. The rooms were two steps down from the foyer and most people tripped when they came in because it was hard to notice them. It took a few days of shopping around until I found the perfect tiles to go on the risers of the two stairs down to the big rooms. A beige tile with a diamond cut out was perfect after I added diamond shaped iridescent glass of burgundy and cobalt blue. It was quite dramatic and gave the place a Spanish feel. Rearranging the old furniture gave the place a sense of style.

I had always hated the window treatments in the master suite. The large mutton barred windows had metal vertical blinds on them that made a racket when the windows were open on a breezy day. They looked out of date, reminiscent of the eighties. I still liked the paint job on the walls. The color was called urban sky and it was the color of a hazy city on a summer day with a few clouds. The sand colored carpet and the sea gulls that hung on the walls made the room feel like walking on the beach. The black furniture was still very modern. It was the windows that were all wrong. I glitzed them up with new white wooden blinds and white sheers with sparkles all over them. The rods of black iron with a crystal ball on either end held sheers and valances I made myself. When the sun shines in the room sparks fly everywhere.

The redecorating was completed by the day of the party held at the condo's club house. Zev and his band played great music for my ninety-five guests and family members that came for dinner. People talked about it for months after. I enjoyed my days of leisure but I kept thinking about my patients. I wondered how they were getting along in the nursing homes. "I'm only one person!" I reminded myself out loud. I couldn't do anything on my own to help them. I knew and understand the power of words. I saw, firsthand, how they could change people, make them see things differently. Words made them think and feel things. I was then, and still am, a great reader of all kinds of books, fiction and non-fiction. Novels and the people who write them have always made me wonder how they can just make up a story. After exploring more I realized that there is more truth in novels than any other form of the written word. In a novel you can say anything you want, tell the most intimate details of life and speak truths that may otherwise never be spoken. Through fiction you can discover a lot about yourself and others. I began to think that writing novels about my experiences might be fun but also a way of ridding my conscience of all the pain and suffering I've seen over the years. I thought I could find peace and comfort in my old age by getting to know myself.

Writing is difficult. Sometimes, what makes sense one day makes none the next. Putting your thoughts down on paper requires that you expose yourself to criticism. Knowing yourself helps. When I started writing my memoirs after I retired seven years ago, I found that just compiling them was not enough. I had to make a story out of them, something interesting that people would want to read. I began to conduct informal interviews with old friends and co-workers I had known throughout my life and my career. I was surprised to learn that some of those I met with remembered the same things. They felt the same way about a lot of the things that had occurred in our lives over the years.

I met with Guadalupe Hernandez on a beautiful early fall day. We met in the old part of South Side at a Mexican restaurant we both loved. "Lupe, do you remember much about the early days when we first worked together?" I asked.

"Oh, I guess I can remember lots of things from back then. What specifically?" she asked.

"Well, I remember when we were introduced and started to work together. You didn't like me much I could tell.

You never said it but I could feel it. I knew I liked you right away. I wanted very much to impress you and learn from you as well."

"Yes, that's right Mary; I didn't like you very much because you were so sure of yourself. I felt that you thought you knew everything. I guess now I see that you were trying to impress me and win me over as well as increase your knowledge. But, yes, you were a real pain back then." She said and we both had a good laugh over those memories.

We had grown children and we were both crazy for our grand-children. They bring us such great joy. It's the kind of happiness that we didn't get to experience with our own children when they were growing up. I think it was because we were trying to be all things to all people. We were the new generation going forward. We wanted to make our mark in the work place. We wanted to be heard and to make the work place better for all women who wanted to enter it. Most of us were like Lupe and me, Suzanne and Sheila. We worked because we had to work.

We had husbands who didn't bring in enough money for us to live the life we wanted for ourselves and our children. We wanted a better life for our kids than we had growing up. We wanted a more just world for them. We were pioneers of the women's movement although we didn't truly know it then. When I look at the world today, it seems so even though I hear some of the most bewildering statements come out of the mouths of public officials in high places. Women still make less money than men in the same jobs. There has never been a woman President. Women do more than sixty percent of all domestic tasks and most of the child rearing. Politicians have learned to just pat us on the back and say "Good job" without giving us higher offices or better pay.

After spending these last seven years remembering, writing and interviewing my old friends, I began to wonder where my sense of justice for all, my deep caring about the welfare of others around me came from. I've written about the struggles of my parents who came to a foreign land to raise their children in a better world. I used to wonder why they struggled so hard for so little. Prompted by this deep desire to trace my parent's heritage, I thought the best way to learn was to go back to where they had been born and raised. I had been to Australia and had visited the places where my father's three brothers had settled when they left Italy in the early 1930's. It was easy to see why they went there and stayed. What I really wanted to know was why they all left Italy to travel half way around the world in search of higher ground so to speak.

Elizabeth Lewis has been my friend since 1978 when we both campaigned for our local congressman. One day I met Elizabeth and her friend Nelda Amati for lunch. They're retired teachers. Nelda was born in Italy and came to the states when she was just thirteen. He parents gave her a good education and she became a professor of English. She still owned her childhood home in the south of Italy. Elizabeth's grandmother had come to the US as a ten year old girl. She recalled many happy hours at her grandmother's table hearing stories about the small town in the mountains of southern Italy. "I have always longed to see that small village." Elizabeth confessed to us over lunch.

"Well, why don't you and Mary come and visit me in my town of San Lugido?" Nelda asked. "You could visit that village as it is not far from me." It sounded like such a wonderful idea that we began to plan our trip abroad. I would visit my parents little town of Sinagra, Sicily and Elizabeth would finally get to see the place of her grandmother's many stories.

In order to really understand how you got to where you are, I realized, you have to know how and why you got there in the first place. A journey to the old country was just what we longed for now that we were retired. We wanted to have a deeper understanding of ourselves, our ambitions and the paths in life we had chosen to walk.

Chapter 17

Return To Sinagra, Where No One A Stranger

When I was born in the early forties my father was over fifty and my mother was thirty-six. They were more like grandparents by the standards of their time. Men and women married at much younger ages and had children right away. This age gap between us had been a hindrance and a help to me all my life. I lived at home with them until I was almost twenty-two. When they spoke to me in Italian I answered them in English. I made little or no effort to learn to speak their language. They spoke enough English to make themselves understood in their adopted homeland. The stories they told of their little town I always considered some sort of fairytale. I never felt it was actual truth. I thought of it as their way of entertaining us as children. I often wondered why they never went back if it was such a great place. I went so far as to ask them on more than one occasion. The answer was always the same for both of them. "We wanted better lives for you kids, opportunity for education and employment. Jobs, any jobs in Italy were hard to come by."

Once when I was in grade school, my mother went back to Sinagra. She was gone for four months. Nine years later, my parents made the trip back together and stayed three months. They seemed very glad to be home on the farm when they returned even though it was evident that they had enjoyed the visit. My own curiosity about Sinagra began to grow after my retirement. As an adult, I had stopped asking questions about Italy. I had forgotten many of the stories of the old country. Life happens and you just have to go with the flow of it. I went to nursing school got a job and moved out of my parent's home. Then I got married and had two children while life changed in ways I never expected. After my husband left the family, I realized that I would have to go back to school for a higher degree in order to support my girls. I wanted to send them to the best schools. I wanted better for them just as my parents had wanted for me and my siblings. I wanted private schools and university educations for them. During those hard years, I am ashamed to admit, I saw little of my parents as they advanced in years. I struggled to keep a home and educate my own children.

Once I could work less, be finished with school and sleep at night, I thought I would sit down with my mother and father and make a recording of all their stories of Italy where they grew up. Once again life got in the way. I found myself working harder than ever before in a very high stress job as a nurse practitioner in a private cardiology practice as well as holding a part time job. I was in the Army Nurse Corp Reserves as an officer. My older daughter was in college and her younger sister was in a private high school. As the bills rolled in, I could see no way out of the life I was living. Then my father's health began to fail and it wasn't long before he died at the ripe old age of ninety-six. Two years later I found myself facing my own mortality as the diagnosis of the first cancer I had was given me. I battled my own health problems over the next ten years while still trying to get my daughters through college. Then I financed cars for them and made sure they were capable of caring for themselves as I was uncertain I would be there in the future. During those trying times my mother became more withdrawn and started to show signs of dementia. She died in the year 2000 and I had never gotten the chance to record those stories. It is one of the deepest regrets of my life.

I set out on a quest to rediscover Sinagra. I wanted to understand where I came from and why I hold so dear my beliefs and convictions. I held a great curiosity about the elderly and where they came from, what their lives were once like. A lot of health care providers don't share my love or my desire to give them the best the world has to offer. "My but I really hate working on a floor where there is a bunch of those old folks." A fellow nurse said one day. "They are so demanding and they fuss over every little thing! They're such a drag."

"Did you ever stop to think that maybe it's all they have left? Perhaps it is the only way they can get any attention or get someone to talk to them. They have lost control over their own lives and little things make them feel they can still be a vital part of life" I said.

"Well I suppose that's true but they're so irritating, boring and I really don't like listening to them." She replied.

"We all come from elderly people don't we?" I asked. "I bet your mother is getting older and I know you have a grandmother. I'm sure she had a mother too. What do you know of them and how they relate to you and your life? Why don't you ask and find out? I think you will be surprised and pleased to learn of your heritage." I don't know if that nurse ever took my advice. I felt it was time to take my own advice and return to the home of my ancestors.

My friend Elizabeth Lewis and I decided to take Nelda's offer of a visit to her beloved San Lugido in Calabria Italy. This village of about seven thousand is located on the Mediterranean Sea. It is beautiful as if right out of a travel log. On the flight over Elizabeth began to school me on the Italian language. Being a retired Spanish teacher, it appealed to her. She had been studying the Italian language for about four years. While it is similar to Spanish, the two are not exactly the same. She had been to Italy many times. She always relied on her Spanish in order to navigate the country. Although it had served her well in the past, she longed to be able to communicate in Italian. "Ok, Mary, we will commence to learn to communicate in Italian for the duration of our trip." Elizabeth instructed. We were on Alitalia Air and they all speak it. She tried teaching me phrases I was sure I would never need to utter while in country. I could see no benefit to being able to say "I have hemorrhoids" or "I am in need of contraception" in Italian. I found myself slipping into the same pattern of behavior with Elizabeth as I had with my parents. As she spoke Italian, I answered her in English. "Now come on Mary you have to say it in Italian!" she demanded. For nine hours of air time I tried my best.

Nelda and her cousin were waiting for us when we arrived in Lamezsia, Calabria. We drove very fast down the coast of the Mediterranean. The scenery took my breath away, it was so beautiful. I felt as if I was in a travel documentary. As the days went by, we explored the little town and we discovered that no one spoke English other than our hostess. I was surprised that my Italian came out fairly easy. We went into little shops and made friends with the owners who were all more than glad to help us and visit with us. We sat at sidewalk cafés and ate pizza, gelato and fresh pasta made just that very day. I hadn't expected the stifling heat and the lack of air conditioning and good plumbing. What really amazed me was people get up early in the morning and shop for the food they needed for the day. They started their day with a cappuccino and a pastry called a cornetti. It looks like a crescent, but wasn't not greasy or flakey. It was more like yeast bread filled with different jellies and jams or nutella and cream. When the one o'clock hour came everything shuts down and everyone went inside to sleep until about five or six o'clock. It was the hottest time of day and closing up to sleep was how they coped without air conditioning.

In the evening the town came alive again as people strolled along the piazza visiting with one another while children play. Shops opened and people dined el fresco. No one was home in front of the TV or the computer. They were all interacting with each other. There was no separation of classes or age groups. The business men and women visited with the cab drivers, the polizzia (police) were everywhere as the street sweepers swept. We visited tobacco shops and bars where mountains of information can be found. If you need anything you can find it in those places. Smoking was everywhere, but in Italy they all smoked out of doors. We visited a tobacco store where the owners helped us figure out how to get to the respective birth places of our people. The wife was educated in the states and she knew English well. I was anxious to get to Sicily and Elizabeth wanted to see her grandmother's birth place of Alto Monte. Ida was a wealth of information about how to get to the places we longed to visit. She sent us to a travel agent in the nearby town of Paola. We went there on the bus. It cost each of us one euro which was about one dollar and twenty-five cents. The agency was located right in the town square. It was very easy to find in the quaint little sea side city that had wonderful shops and candy stores. The agency was run by a husband and wife team. Although they seemed to argue a lot they ran the place well. They were very helpful and it seemed they couldn't do enough for us. We discovered they both loved America and had cousins they visited often who live quite near me.

"So you want to go to Sicily?" Fredo said. "Look how easy it is. You will get the train right here in Paola and it will take you directly to Capo D' Orlando which is right on the Sicilian coast. The Hotel IL Molino is right on the beach and it has a four star rating. From there it is only 18 kilometer to Sinagra. You could take a taxi."

"Does it have Air conditioning?" I asked using my best Italian.

"Yes and the breakfasts are included in the price of eighty euros per night, a wonderful price." He replied. I was excited and couldn't wait to go.

"Where will I need to go to catch the train?" I asked.

"You will come here in the morning and I will take you there myself." I must have had a very skeptical look on my face and everything I was thinking at that moment must have been printed right on my forehead.

Fredo's wife then spoke up, "We do this for all of our customers. It is our pleasure to escort you and make sure you know where you are going."

All I could do was mutter a grateful "Grazzi tonto," which meant, "Thank you very much".

Although Elizabeth's Alto Monte was only about an hour and fifteen minutes away, we soon learned that it would be more difficult for her to travel there than it was for me to go from Calabria to Sicily. There was no bus or train to take her. There was no taxi service in the small city of Paola that we could hire to drive her. The village, located in the mountains, although well known to many around the world, had limited access to it. The decision for each of us to visit our own respective villages was made even before we left the states. Since we knew our time was limited, we hadn't any idea how long the journeys would take so we decided to split up for that portion of our trip.

That evening, after packing for my two day stay in Sicily, I faced a sad and unhappy Elizabeth. She had her heart set on going to Alto Monte. I was sad for her. When we walked to the piazza that evening, a group of men sitting at an outdoor café asked if we were finding everything alright. We asked them if they knew a taxi driver who would drive Elizabeth to her destination. They said that they could find us someone if we were interested. They thought it might cost one hundred euros. Elizabeth told them she would let them know. I knew she wasn't sure that taking advice from a group of men out in the street was such a good idea.

We went to the Tobacco shop to see Ida and tell her thanks for the information about the travel agency. She expressed her regret that they were unable to help Elizabeth find a way to her village. We walked down to our favorite place to get a cornetti. Two young people were working in the shop. We told them Elizabeth couldn't get a taxi to her village. The young girl told us her father spoke good English and could help us. He lived upstairs from the little shop. We took our treats and sat outside to wait for Jon Carlo. We learned quickly that time to an Italian means very little, five minutes could be an hour or more.

Finally, Jon Carlo appeared but he spoke little English, although he had spent some years working in the states. We explained Elizabeth's dilemma to him. He gave us the same taxi number that we had seen in the shop. We told him we had the number but we were reluctant to call. "I will do it for you and I will have Ugo (Italian for Hugo) come here and talk to you." In less than fifteen minutes an older gentleman in a Mercedes van pulled up to the shop. He was very pleasant and friendly. He seemed to be quite close friends with Jon Carlo our shop owner. He was very agreeable with the plan to take Elizabeth to her village. We, however, were still a little unsure. We began to explain to him and Jon Carlo where we were staying and with whom. They both seemed to know Nelda very well. Ugo offered to drive us home. Reluctantly we got into the Mercedes. He began flying through the streets of San Lugido. We became a little nauseated and disoriented to say the least. Suddenly we were right in front Nelda's house! "See I told you I know her." He said.

Nelda was on the balcony. She was a little more than irritated with us for getting in a car with a man we didn't know. "But he knows you, Nelda, he drove us right here without any instructions from us." I said in defense of our impulsive actions.

"That doesn't mean I know him or approve of him." she said. For the first time in a long time, I felt like an errant teenager explaining to my parents where I had been and with whom. I couldn't understand where Nelda was coming from. Surely she knew we were both grown women and would not hold her responsible for our welfare while we were here in Italy.

"I've been here many times." Ugo said. "I drove the girls here for the wedding you hosted last year. Don't you remember me? I'm Luigi's cousin by marriage." Once Nelda was assured that she knew Ugo and that was a reliable driver, she didn't object to his taking Elizabeth. I was sure Ugo was quite elderly; he spoke of his wife and grandchildren. He told us that he and his wife had just celebrated there fiftieth wedding anniversary. With all arrangements for our respective adventures made, Elizabeth and I retired to our lavish quarters on the second floor of Nelda's home for a good night's sleep. We would both be going on our trips over the weekend.

There were many people about that Friday morning. The sun was already hot as I set out for the bus stop. I felt confident that I knew how to take the bus to Paola and get myself back to the travel agency. The bus stopped right in the town square by a big fountain. Eight o'clock turned into nine and then nine-thirty but no bus came. I began to get very nervous and scared as the heat intensified. Then at ten minutes before ten a bus going to Paola came down the street. I told the driver in my best Italian that I wanted to go to IV November. You could not imagine my shock when he told me the bus didn't go there on Friday. "But how will I get there?" I asked, starting to panic a little. He explained he would let me off at his last stop and show me how I could walk there. "Is it far?" I ask. He told me that it was far but he thought I could walk it. To my surprise he stopped the bus at the top of a hill and pointed down a very narrow street that looked more like an alley. He told me to walk down it and turn left at the end. I would see the town square and IV November was just beyond it. I took my bag and walked down the crowded way. No one paid me much attention. I was a little relieved. The town square was not immediately visible when I turned the corner causing panic to rise in my stomach. Two ladies were standing out in front of a bar. I asked them how to get to the travel agency. One of them smiled and indicated with her hand that I only needed to walk a short distance and I would see it. I was soon in front of the agency as relief flooded over me.

I checked the time and realized that it had taken me only twenty minutes to get there since boarding the bus. I was quite early! I went to a bar across the street and got a bottle of ice cold water. I sat at a table on the side walk and began to drink, cooling myself. Everyone looked my way. They asked if I was enjoying myself and if I was finding everything I needed. I was amazed they knew I wasn't a local. They knew I was an American. I responded to them in the best Italian I could articulate. Paola is a good sized bustling place with many shops and lots of people. They were all Italians who did not speak English. It was a place so very different from anywhere in America. All the people, both young and old, spoke to me. Everyone was friendly. The young in our country seem to only want to talk to each other and most never even notice an elderly person. If you stop them to ask directions they may answer you politely but hurry on their way barely looking in your direction. Everyone there looked you in the eyes and asked about your wellbeing before continuing the conversation. They took care to give you direction. There seems to be a respect for older people here that I have never seen or experienced anywhere in the Americans.

Gentlemen make way for you as you pass them on the street or offer you their seat on the bus if you are standing. No one appears to be in too big a hurry to be polite and friendly.

"You are here! You have plenty of time before you have to catch your train. It does not leave until noon." Fredo said when I arrived at the agency. We settled the bill and I got my tickets to and from Capo D' Orlando. They were all written in Italian of course. I sat waiting anxiously while he answered the telephone and waited on other customers who came into the agency. It was quite a busy place. I began to wonder if we would make that train on time. Fredo was relaxed and attentive. As I waited an idea came into my head. I wrote down my home address and phone number and gave it to him. Speaking as clearly as I could, I told him that when he and his family came to America he could call me. I would get them from the airport and take them to his cousin who lived only about a half hour from me. It would be my way of repaying him for his kindness and attention.

It occurred to me that it was my first time traveling in a foreign land all alone. Although I had done well thus far using my limited knowledge of Italian, I had no idea how I would manage in Sicily. At ten minutes before the hour Fredo said, "Come we go now." We got into his Fiat and went only a few blocks to the train station. He took me right to the track for my coach and told me to get on the coach numbered five only as it would be the one that would go all the way to my destination. He kissed me on both cheeks European style and said "Good-bye with instructions that I was to return to see him as soon as I got back and tell him how I had fared.

As I waited patiently for the train that was obviously late, I began to see that it was not easy to tell one coach from another. Panic began again at a more intense level. It took a while to recognize the station attendants. They were dressed in light blue shirts and navy blue pants with a very small insignia on the shirt pocket. I approached one of them, showed my ticket and asked about the train, the right coach. I told him I was an American here for the first time. He chuckled and said that I probably would never return to the region again. "Oh no!" I replied "I like it here very much, it is so beautiful. All of the people are friendly, kind and so helpful." He blushed and thanked me saying that he was glad to hear it as most Americans didn't like the south of Italy. He said that they found it too primitive and basic not luxurious enough for them.

When the train finally arrived he made sure I was on the right coach. The scenery that flashed by as the train sped along was so wonderful I couldn't take my eyes off it. I hardly noticed the others in my car but they appeared to be mostly men traveling on business, most had computers and cell phones. I was feeling better. It was tolerable in the coach but again the air conditioning was not as cool as I had hoped it would be.

Even though the train was late we seemed to be making good time. It wasn't long before we got to the sea and to the ferry that would take the train across to the island of Sicily. The cars seemed to be rolling back and forth for some time. It grew darker and then it seemed that the engine of the train stopped all together. The heat began to rise in the car and it became quite uncomfortable. I asked the woman who was sitting across from me where I might find a bathroom. She indicated the rear of the car but then said that I would not be able to use it now because the train was turned off while we were inside the ferry going across the sea. She assured me that I could go up on the top of it, use the bathroom, get something to drink and look around. I was too unsure of myself, so I just sat there wondering when the train would start up again as it was due to arrive in Capo D' Orlando at around five-fifteen. Then the lady asked me if I would like an espresso. I politely declined her offer as she smiled and turned to go. When she returned she handed me the coffee and said that she hoped I would enjoy it. I thanked her and I did enjoy it, very much.

She started to read a book. I continued my vigil at the window. An hour had passed before the train started to move again. It was slow at first and then we emerged into sun shine brightness. The air was functioning again. I was excited and moved by the sign that indicated we were in Messina because I knew my parents had been there many times. They had talked of its beauty often when I was a girl. I felt close to my roots and to my parents as the train stopped again I felt a little emotional. Regret flooded through me that I hadn't been the most attentive child when I had the chance to learn more about their beautiful homeland.

I was snapped out of my musing when I heard the lady across from me ask a gentlemen who was about to get off the train, if he would please lift her suitcase for her from overhead. It was too large for her and she was going all the way to Capo D' Orlando and there would be no one to help her after he left the car. When the gentleman had left, I told the lady that I, too, was going to that destination.

I explained to her that I was an American seeking to find my parents' hometown which was nearby. I wasn't sure what made me so talkative but I told her that I was alone on this adventure and that I had never been to Sicily.

While pulling her own suitcase, she took my bag and my arm and said, "You will come with me. I will help you find your way." Before I knew it, we were off the train and on the sidewalk outside the station. She told me her name was Tina. I told her mine. Still holding my arm, she yelled for someone named Gino who seemed to appear out of nowhere. He took my bag and put me in the back seat of his car. It all happened so suddenly, I began to wonder if I should start to worry about getting in cars with complete strangers. He asked me where I was staying. I told him the Hotel IL Molino. He indicated that it was only a few blocks away. I protested saying I could walk there, but he insisted on driving me. When he pulled up in front of the hotel, not wanting to inconvenience them further, I got out quickly and thanked them for their help. But the man took my bag; he and Tina followed me into the hotel.

They made sure I secured my room. When Tina told him I wanted to go to Sinagra to see if I could find some of my relatives there Gino wanted to know the names of the persons I was seeking. He immediately recognized the name. He gave me his number told me to call him in the morning. He would see if he could get away to drive me there. I took his number and the desk clerk gave him the number of the hotel as well. I just couldn't thank them enough.

After I was settled in my room, I realized I hadn't eaten since breakfast. I went down to the front desk and asked the clerk if there was a place that she could recommend for a good meal, the conversation was entirely in Italian. Capo D' Orlando is a resort town for Italians; no American tourists visited the area. She gave me a strange look and asked, "You mean you want to eat now?" She turned to the clock on the wall and noted the time; it was only five-forty-five. I was starving! I told her, yes, I most certainly want to eat right then, although the dinner hour was much later. She sent me to the end of the block where there was a sidewalk café that would accommodate me.

When I walked out of the lobby, I was taken by surprise to be facing the Ionian Sea! It was the most beautiful place I had ever seen. The water was so clear and it changed colors every few minutes with the movement of the afternoon sun. I walked across the street. I was literally right on the beach at the water's edge. It made me dizzy and my breath caught, it was so magnificent. I walked along until I came to the outdoor café. There was a young man at the counter who asked how he could help me. I told him I was from America, I didn't speak the language well but I wished to order something to eat. He immediately turned to all of his guests seated by the sea side. He announced I was from American and here for my first visit. They all stood up and cheered loudly. I had never experienced anything like that in my life! I was both embarrassed and amazed at the attention. The café was filled with mostly young people. Some were with families and there was a whole soccer team having afternoon drinks. They all came over and wished me well expressing their desire that I have a good stay in their beautiful seaside town.

The gentleman at the counter, who couldn't have been more than thirty, seated me at a table and told me he would bring me food. I had street pizza, which is very easy to pick up and eat with your hands, cold bottled water, a cappuccino and, of course, a large gelato. Sicily is noted for it and other sweet treat. It was like no other ice cream I had ever tasted in Italy or America. My young waiter charged me only four euros for the meal which is about five dollars in American money. I mused that I could not think of any place in the states where you could get such a meal for that price. I had never experienced such friendliness in a town of complete strangers. As I walked back to the hotel along the beach, everyone I passed said hello no matter if they were man, woman or child.

That night I slept in the comfort and luxury of a fine air conditioned room for the first time since arriving in Italy. I cranked it up so high that I had to sleep covered with a blanket. It felt so good and I slept well even though many people were out and about. All through the night there was laughter, talking, music and joy which, for the Italian people, are the purpose of the night time hours. I fell into a deep sleep, dreamed of Sinagra and meeting my distant cousins. I wasn't sure who I would find there. I hoped I would be able to meet someone who knew of my parents and their life. My brother had given me names of people he had met there more that twenty-five years ago when he had taken my father back for a visit. That trip had been a long time ago, before he became too unfit for travel. Those he and my father had visited were very old at that time. I was sure that most, if not all, would no longer be living. My brother Marco had no phone numbers or addresses for any of them only directions on how to find the store my first cousin owned. He assured me that she would know me and be able to introduce me to the others.

I was up early the next morning and very anxious to be on my way to Sinagra. I had a good breakfast in the dining room of the hotel which was included in the price of my room. Unfortunately there was no air conditioning in that beautifully decorated room. The meal consisted of a buffet with cold meats, cheeses, hard boiled eggs and Panini breads, fresh fruits and juices. There was the biggest display of sweets I had ever seen in one place. There was, of course, all the cappuccino you could drink. Everyone said good morning as they passed by my table. It appeared that they were a tour group there for some kind of retreat or seminar. They all filed out of the dining room into a meeting hall at the other end of the lobby where they commenced to enjoy music and speeches of some sort.

It took me a while to figure out how to use the phone. I called Tina and Gino whom I had met the day before. Unfortunately they were unable to take me to Sinagra due to some family problem that needed their attention. They couldn't express enough how sorry they were that they couldn't help me. I went ahead with my original plan to hire a taxi to take me there. I knew it wasn't far from where I was staying. I told the clerk where I wished to go and asked her if she could find a taxi to take me. She made a phone call and inquired how much it would cost for a driver to take me there and then return for me in the afternoon. She wrote on a piece of paper that it would cost sixty euros. It was a good price and I told her to order the cab. My anxiety and excitement grew as I recalled the conversation I had with my daughter the night before about my plans to get to Sinagra. "I think what you are doing is quite dangerous Mother! You don't know any of these people and it could end in disaster." I assured her that I would be very careful. I would phone her when I returned to the hotel after my excursion. With my bag packed full of small gifts for any cousins I might meet in Sinagra, I waited in the lobby for the taxi. It was steaming hot already at nine-thirty in the morning as I sat on a white Italian leather sofa. Beads of sweat were forming on my forehead and upper lip. Dabbing at my face with a Kleenex from my bag, I looked up to see a tall, darkly handsome man enter the lobby and walk to the desk. He spoke softly to the desk clerk who nodded in my direction. He approached wishing me a good morning and bent to pick up my bag. He escorted me to his waiting car which was a very small dark green Fiat with a dented fender on the passenger's side in the back. I felt my anxiety climb as the car didn't resemble what I was expecting a taxi to look like. A yellow tag on the front visor caught my eye as he settled me in the back seat. I read with my limited ability with written Italian, it was a license for a cab.

When he came to a mountain road and began flying down it quickly, it was the first time that I realized how high up we were although we were right on the sea. I felt a little nausea as I looked out the window then I noticed him checking me out in the rear view mirror. He quickly looked away. I smiled and boldly kept looking at his handsome face in that same mirror. When our eyes met once again he spoke politely and said in Italian, "Signora, pore favor, you are alone are you not?"

"Why, yes I most certainly am alone." I answered him in the best Italian I could muster up. He shook his head and seemed to become a little more than flustered. "What is your name sir, if I may ask?"

"It is Maurizio." He said still stealing disapproving looks at me in the rear view mirror.

"Well, Maurizio, my name is Maria and I am pleased to make your acquaintance. As you can see I am an old woman. I feel quit safe traveling alone. No one here wants to harm an elder person on holiday. Besides I've lived my life, so far, to the fullest. So if anything happens to me, I really don't mind because I will die doing what I want to do. I won't be doing it in some old folk's home back in America."

"If you are from America why you are here on holiday instead of going where the Americans go when they come to Italia?" he asked.

"I wish to go to Singara because it is the town where my parents were born, grew up, met and married. They left it and went to America in 1929 to give their children a better life. I am the youngest of those children. I want to see where they lived. I want to see if I can find any of my cousins or anyone who would remember them. I want to visit the graves of my grandparents and my uncles and aunts. You see, I have worked hard all my life as a single mother of two and a grandmother of five. I worked as a doctor back in the states." I would never have elevated myself to such a level but Nelda had explained to me that there were no advanced practice nurses in Southern Italy. The closest to explaining to them what it was I had done for a living would be family practice physician which is entry level there. Other countries are more advanced in Europe and employ many advanced practice nurses in England, France and Germany. They are also common in Australia as well.

He continued to shake his head but he had a little smile and he asked, "Do any of your people know you are coming and do you have an address of where they live?"

"The answer to your questions is no, I don't have any addresses, only names and directions to where I might find them. No they do not know I am coming." I replied with confidence that I didn't really possess.

Laughing a little now he inquired "Then this is a surprise?"

"Yes it is. Tell me, Maurizio, are you married and do you have a family?" I asked. I truly wanted to know a little more about my handsome driver, since he had managed to get me to blab all about myself to him in my not so well spoken Italian. I had noticed that he was a little more than amused at times with some of my pronunciations. He told me that he was married with two sons who were now twenty and twenty-four. Although he looked much younger I gaged his age to be about forty-five.

A few minutes had passed in silence when he pulled the cab off the road and said, "This is Sinagra." I looked franticly out one back window at a grassy hill and then the other window faced a pebble beach some distance away.

"Where is it? I cannot see anything that looks like a town." He began pointing up as I looked at him in utter confusion. He rolled down the window to my left and said again to look out and up. I put my head through the window and looked up onto a beautiful little mountain town built straight up into it! When I was a child, my mother always told me that she came from a town that was built right into the side of a mountain and that, in summer, she swam in the sea. I never took her stories of Sinagra seriously. I thought they were only made up to entertain me and my siblings. The sight of that little town now took my breath away. "How will I ever get up there?" I asked. Maurizio began to laugh and said that he was going to take me there but he needed to know where it was I wanted to go exactly. "Well to the town square, of course, to the piazza. I will look for my cousin's store from there." He again looked at me with doubt in his eyes as we pulled back onto the highway.

When he stopped the cab in the town square, I started to get out and hand him the money. He immediately instructed me to sit firmly there in the back seat. He would go and talk to the police who was there in the square. I watched and listened as he inquired as to where I could find my cousin whose name I had given him when we first set out on this adventure. I felt excited and anxious as I waited for him to finish speaking to the officer. "Yes I know just who it is that the signora is looking for. His name is Nino and he owns a store right here on this block. I will go and find him for you." I waited patiently in the taxi but my heart was pumping wildly.

I saw the two men enter the square at the far end of the street. The officer gestured toward the cab as he spoke. The man was in his late forties or early fifties. I could see a family resemblance to my mother's people. The man who was called Nino approached the cab. He looked at me through the open window and stated that he had never seen me before in his life. He didn't know what it was I wanted with him. I knew then that I had to get out and state my case for coming there as best I could. Maurizio stood by ready to aid me if I needed him. I did my best to explain to Nino who I was and why I had come so far. It took a few minutes but then he realized that we were indeed cousins' even if distant ones. I inquired after my first cousin Serena who had the store at the end of the block. I was very disappointed to learn that she was in her mid-eighties and suffering from Alzheimer's disease. He told me she no longer recognized anyone and was being cared for in a nursing facility. She had closed the little grocery store twenty years ago. She had been living with failing health since. "What about the farm?" I asked.

"May I go and see it? Who is living there now if Serena is in a nursing home?"

"I am sorry to say that the farm is no longer in the family. I don't believe it is a farm anymore. I must apologize as I have no more time to visit with you. I am alone in the store and must get back to my customers." He said with genuine regret.

"Where is the cemetery?" I asked. "I would like to visit the graves of my cousin Carlo and my grandmothers." "It is not far only a short distance away." He explained to Maurizio and then he turned to me and said, "Do you know Carlo Jr.? He lives in New York City. He is quite prominent in the government there. Why don't you contact him for more information about your cousins? Most of the names you have on this list are deceased and their offspring no longer live here in Sinagra." I thanked him for his time and gave him one of the gifts I had brought from America. He turned a walked by to his shop which was a men's clothing store a very short distance from the piazza.

"Come, I will take you to the cemetery." Maurizio said as he held open the cab door for me. Just as the town was built into the side of the mountain so was the cemetery which was right around the corner from the small village. It was amazing to see! I tried to exit the taxi quickly as I was excited to see it in all its wondrous beauty. Once again Maurizio prevented me from leaving the cab. "No! You will sit here while I go and find the attendant. He will guide us to your grandmothers' graves." He climbed the mountain with ease in the white hot sun of the approaching afternoon. I listened intently as he inquired after the grave of my grandmother, my mother's mother. The attendant replied quickly pointing to a large cement slab that was a twelve by twelve foot square.

"No no!" I exclaimed getting out of the cab. I began telling the man who was, as he stood many steps above me on the mountain, that my grandmother was buried in a grave with a large black marble headstone that had her picture on it. "I'm sure of it." I protested but he continued to indicate that she was buried in the big cement square near where I was standing. "But I've seen many pictures of it and I know it has to be here somewhere on the ground." The man turned to Maurizio and explained that when families no longer come to visit the grave site of a loved one, they are removed from the ground. They are not buried very deep because after all Sicily is an island. They then transfer them to one mass grave and keep careful records of where everyone is placed.

I couldn't remember ever being more moved, disappointed and emotionally spent all at once. Maurizio and I walked about the graves most of them were names I knew from childhood. I understood that they were all related to me in some way from the stories my mother told me. There was a chief officer of the Carbinari which is the police for the whole country of Italy. Maurizio explained to me that cousin of mine had been a powerful man. I spotted my cousin Carlo Sr.'s grave and went to it. Almost everyone has their picture on their grave so they are easy to locate. Maurizio noted that my cousin's wife was still alive. He asked if I wanted to locate her. He thought that since there were fresh flowers on his grave that she must still live in the village. "I'm afraid she lives in New York with the son and his family. I'm not sure who puts flowers on Carlo's grave." I said. I looked up and saw there in the side of the mountain my other grandmother's grave. Her name was there in big gold letters with her picture. I knew that stern face well as it hangs on a wall in the entrance to my condo. The picture is a large oval one of her and my mother when she became engaged to my father. I called out to the attendant and asked him why my father's mother was still buried there when she had died many years before my other grandmother.

"We only move the ones that are in the ground, Signora, not those who are in the mountain they will remain there always." He replied. So my Grandmother Lenzo was in a vault inside the mountain! The sun had become very hot and I felt very over heated and tired. We thanked the attendant. I was disappointed as we made our way back to the taxi.

"Where would you like to go now?" Maurizio asked once we were on the road again. "To an ATM machine, I think." I replied.

"Do you mean you want to go to a bank?" He asked. I assured him that that was exactly what I wanted to do. After withdrawing some cash I got back in the cab. "Where shall I take you now? Do you wish to stay here until the afternoon as you had planned or do you wish to return to Capo D' Orlando?"

"I think I will return as there seems to be no one else I can visit." I said feeling the full weight of my regret.

"Come we will take our time going back and you can get some pictures." He said noting the camera still in my hand. I took many shots of Sinagra and a few of Maurizio too. We stopped here and there to take in the sights of the sea. As I looked down from the mountain I could remember my mother's stories of the times she had gone swimming in the sea. It was so magnificent. I was sure it had been that very spot. How I longed again to have recorded some of those conversations with her and my father those many years ago.

In front of the hotel I leaned over and handed Maurizio one hundred and fifty euros. He first looked stunned and then gave me a scowl as if insulted. "Maurizio, don't argue with me. You have spent many hours with me when you could have been getting other fairs. Tell me, are you working tomorrow?" I asked. He replied that he had to work every day in order to make ends meet. "Fine, then you will take me to the train in the morning around say eleven o'clock? You will get me on the right train and coach back to Calabria. We will get to say good-bye again."

He shook his head and smiled at me. At that moment, I could read his mind. He was thinking, 'those crazy American'! He agreed to the plan as he extended his hand to me.

It felt good to be back in my air conditioned room. I was tired and most likely had suffered a little altitude sickness, but it didn't occur to me at the time. I looked out at the sea and the Isle of Leona came into view as once again the waters turned every color under the sun. I lie down on the bed and fell into a deep sleep for a few hours. I woke suddenly to the roar of waves. I looked out and saw the water crashing against the rock and flying into the air as high as the hotel itself. It was a magnificent sight and I longed to walk on the beach again. The sea had turned a deep midnight blue and there were clouds overhead. I could no longer see the Isle of Leona. The wind roared as I walked along getting pelted with sand and tiny pebbles on the beach. It was so beautiful I just didn't want to go inside. I shopped at a novelty store across from the hotel. I walked down to the sidewalk café once again to dine early as I was still on American time and accustomed to eating an early dinner.

The man at the counter and the people there all seemed to remember me from the day before. They were very friendly. The waiter once again fed me way too much. He encouraged me to try another flavor of gelato that he suggested giving me way more than I could eat. I took another walk along the beach. I came to a platform made of colorful tiles. It read Capo D' Orlando founded in 1299 by Captain Molino. The wind was almost too difficult to walk in as I made my way back to the hotel. I was in awe of the fact that I was visiting a town that was so old. We Americans are always so caught up in what is new and modern. I loved visiting somewhere so old. It was somewhere that my parents had been as well.

Even though it had cooled off a lot out doors, it was still stifling hot in the lobby, so I decided against sitting there to people watch. I went back to my room. I called Nelda to let her know that I was back and safe. I told her I would return to her home at around five the next afternoon. I completely forgot to call my daughter and let her know I was ok. I felt so emotionally and physically drained and so full of gelato that I couldn't keep my eyes open. I went to bed and slept through the night, something I rarely did in my entire life.

In the morning the sun was shining once again turning the sea every shade of blue, green and purple found in nature. Big white caps were crashing against the rocks. The Isle of Leona was shimmering in the distance. I went into the dining room and once again ate a hardy breakfast. It was already hotter than I could bear but I wanted to go to mass. I inquired at the desk for directions to the nearest church. It was not even a full block away, just around the corner from the Il

Molino. While village churches are very plain on the outside they are magnificent inside. The way to tell that it is a church from the outside is the presence of many beggars in front of it. The mass, all in Italian, of course, was quite beautiful. I was able to follow along almost as well as if it had been in English.

I hurried back to the hotel to pack and checkout. I realized when I got to the desk that no one seemed in ahurry to have me leave. In hotels in America you will get an itemized bill under your door in the dead of night of the day you are supposed to leave. No such bill appeared under my door that morning. I was not charged for any of the phone calls I made to Nelda. I had used my phone card to call my daughters. The only thing the clerk asked me was what I took from the refrigerator in my room. She took my word that I only had two bottles of water. The bill for two nights and two lavish breakfasts was less than two hundred American dollars. No four star hotel in the states with an ocean view unlike any other with people, who could not do enough for you, would ever be that cheap! I wondered again why Americans didn't come to such a paradise by the sea. As I sat on the front porch waiting for Maurizio, several gentlemen, most quite elderly, tried to give me their seat. I politely refused as it was much cooler to sit on the marble stairs.

Right at eleven, Maurizio came around the corner in his little Fiat waving and sounding the horn. In the front seat was an older man who immediately jumped out and took my bag. He introduced himself as Maurizio's uncle. He had been to America and couldn't tell me enough how much he had loved it. He had been to the Big City by the lake where I lived. He told me he longed to return someday. I asked him to look me up if he ever did make the trip. Before I could finish my conversation with the uncle we were at the train station. They took me to the right track and told me to get on the next train in coach number five only as it would be the one to take me back to Calabria. We said our good-byes. I was sad to be leaving them and the beautiful Capo D' Orlando. I hoped, one day, to return and explore that wonderful place by the sea.

Looking back I wondered why I didn't plan to stay longer and continue to look up other cousins in the area. I didn't buy any flowers to put on the graves of my grandparents. I didn't buy even one post card. A day or so after I returned to Calabria, that dizzy light headed feeling finally left me. My thoughts cleared. I noticed the change in temperature. It had been so hot in Sicily that I thought I would never feel cool again.

Once on the train, I found my seat and settled in for the long four hour ride back. A man in his seventies with his wife of about the same age sat across from me. They both spoke to each other in pleasant voices that seemed to soothe my frayed nerves. Suddenly a young man appeared in the door way and began to speak in a rambling style. I could only catch one or two words that made sense to me. I had no clue what it was he wanted. The woman said to her husband, she didn't understand the man at all. "Well he is asking for a hand out of money so he can buy milk for his babies." The man said. A wave of relief came over me as I thought it was only I who could not understand what he was talking about. He quickly left when the man waved him off.

"I didn't understand anything he said either. I'm an American here for the first time. I thought it was my poor understanding of the language that I couldn't figure out what he was saying." I said to the woman in my best Italian.

"Oh I think you speak quite well. I hope you are enjoying your stay in Italy? I know that you haven't come just for a vacation otherwise you would not be on this train. Most Americans would not be coming to this area to vacation. My name is Ana. My husband and I are pleased to make your acquaintance," Ana said in a voice that welcomed me. I was glad that I was not the only one who didn't understand what the young man was saying. We fell into easy conversation.

"Thank you Ana for your kind words. I came to Sicily to visit the town where my parents were born. I tried to meet some of my distant cousins who still live in the area. I was somewhat unsuccessful in my attempt to do so.

However, I did get to see the town and meet one of them for a brief time." I replied. We talked about my family and theirs as if we were old friends. It made the time go by quickly. When the train made a stop and a young woman got on I hardly noticed her until she spoke telling me that I was in her seat. I apologized and moved to the seat across from her. I was then riding backwards on the train, a position I had hoped to avoid as it made me more than a little nauseated.

I began to take stock of the young woman because she was so unusual looking for a young Italian girl. First of all she must have been at least three hundred pounds. I was a big woman myself, but she was much larger. She was well dressed in black leggings and an orange blouse that flattered her beautiful clear milk white skin and green eyes. Her long medium brown hair was tied back from her face. I followed those lovely eyes of hers as she began to stare out the window until my own rested on where she was looking. Standing on the platform of the train station was a very well built, slender young man with sandy colored hair and smoking hazel eyes. When their gazes met, the most beautiful love story unfolded before me without one word ever being spoken. I felt like an intruder as his eyes were saying "I love you and I will miss you." I saw true regret in them and, in turn, in hers as she seemed to say "Don't forget me until we meet again." She placed her hand on the glass in a soft gesture as if to stroke his cheek from the window. Then she made a sign that I knew meant "Call me." Their eyes remained locked on one another as the train slowly pulled away. I had never been the romantic sort but I was truly moved by the scene. It brought back memories of the love I had once had for the one and only man I had married those many years ago and lost. I took a deep breath and turned to my other traveling car mates. We continued our conversation where we had left off. Their mood, happy and light, lifted me. I hadn't remembered, once again, that I should have brought something to eat with me. My new friends began to pull out their lunch and insisted that I eat a little with them. They gave me a Panini of cheese, Italian salami and fresh tomatoes and a bottle of ice cold water. The young lady took out her own lunch. I was astounded at the amount that she ate. After devouring four sandwiches and a liter of soft drink, she proceeded to eat an entire box of candy bars. Perhaps her man liked a heavy woman. It may have been her way of pleasing him. I recalled that my father and my three brothers always liked their woman to have a little meat on their bones.

When we neared my destination of Paola, the old couple wanted to know if I was sure of my route. Would there be anyone to meet me? I assured them that I knew where I was and that my friends would pick me up. When we said out good byes, I was saddened by the fact that I would probably never see them again. As I immerged from the station, I spotted Ugo and Elizabeth in the big white Mercedes van. I waved with confidence and climbed in, excited to tell them all about my adventure and hear about Elizabeth's experience in Alto Monte.

For the next week, Elizabeth and I, along with Ugo, our trusted driver, toured around Calabria every day visiting a different sea side destination. One was more beautiful than the last. Tropea was, undoubtedly, the most picturesque of places. "I think there have been quite a few American films made here. It's strange that there are no other Americans vacationing in this beautiful place. There must be more of them than just us." Elizabeth said.

"You two go look around and enjoy. I will come and find you after I have parked the car and have had my smoke." Ugo said.

After we had walked through the streets lined with many shops, filled with flowers, fabulous works of art, jewelry and exotic foods, Elizabeth turned to me and said, "Mary it is so crowded here how will Ugo ever find us! I am worried; I don't think it was a good idea to go off on our own."

"Oh Liz, for heaven sakes, look around you, we're the only Americans here who are charging through the streets as if our tails were on fire. If you haven't noticed, we are the only ones jabbering in English! Ugo will have no difficulty locating us. We laughed and laughed then as we walked around buying beautiful things and looking over the edge of the mountain at the deep blue of the sea. True to his word Ugo found us. We stopped at a café and had a wonderful lunch while we continued to look out at the water.

Tropea is noted for its onions which are bell shaped, red and very sweet. I was drawn to a stand where a very handsome man was selling them along with other delicacies of licorice and anise. What attracted me even more than these things was the man's melodious voice. It had the rich resonance of Morgan Freeman as well as the sweetness of an opera tenor. He told us all the details of the products he sold at his open air stand. He gave us samples of them as he spoke. I was mesmerized by him. I kept buying things and so did Liz. Later, on the way back to Nelda's, we both admitted we kept buying so we could listen to his voice in his beautiful native tongue. The products we had purchased turned out to be of the high quality. Nelda was pleased we had done so well without her guidance. She had been under the weather since our arrival and had not been able to go out with us.

It was hard to leave those wonderful places at the end of our second week in Calabria. We were on our way to Rome to visit the Pope and see the sights of that great ancient city. The flight was only about an hour or so but it was, none the less, an ordeal. Kind and ever patient Ugo carried our bags up and down for us. We were acutely aware that were going to miss him an awful lot. He had been our right hand man since finding him at the sea side café on the piazza. We tried to talk him into coming to Rome with us. We had rented large quarters so had plenty of room for him and we were willing to pay his ticket. But, alas, he had a wife, children and many grandchildren who would miss him too much for him to be our personal guide and chauffer in Rome. "Come back next year. I will be here to take you around once again." He said as he saw us onto the plane bound for more adventures.

Seven days in Rome, in a residential hotel, only two blocks from the Vatican, what could possibly go wrong living so close to the Pope? We were a bit surprised, late that same night, when our cab stopped in the street and let us out. The driver pointed to a large gate and said to just ring the bell, someone would come for us. We rang several times. After some time, I began to worry. Many cars were whizzing by us at unbelievable speeds. Finally a man came running out. He said he had been holding the open button for us and asked why we had not entered. I replied that we had no idea that the gate was being opened by him as it gave no sound from within. He couldn't apologize enough for making us wait as he swiftly brought all our bags and us into the court yard. It was a truly enchanting place in the heart of the city. There were full grown trees and lush flowering bushes and plants. The noise of the street dropped to a mild hum after the gate was closed. Our first floor suite was everything it promised to be on the internet. It was spacious and beautiful with great functioning bathrooms and air conditioning that flowed at top efficiency.

The staff of three young men and one head housekeeper buzzed around doing all they could to make us comfortable. They gave us directions and instructions on how to get to all the sights and how to use public transportation. They had been communicating with Liz ever since she had made our reservations back in the spring. They each had sent her an email every week since, telling her how happy they were we were coming, how much they looked forward to meeting us and making our stay a memorable one. Unless you are a VIP, a Celebrity or a very rich person, such service doesn't happen to ordinary people like us in the States.

Each morning we went to the roof top terrace and had an enormous breakfast. As we sat at our table gazing at the Vatican two blocks away, we talked with other guests. Geraldo brought us cup after cup of cappuccino. The hotel people knew how much we liked being so close to the Pope's house. They got us tickets for an audience with the Pontiff. I wasn't much of a fan of Pope Benedict until the day we went to hear him speak. Attending an audience was quite an experience! We went through the metal detectors, removed our shoes, then through x-ray machines more elaborate than at the airport. There must have been at least sixty thousand people there that day standing in the long line with the heat beating down on us. I started to regret our decision to visit. Once passed security, we were met by the Swiss Guards who have been with the Pope since the time of Michelangelo. They still wear the same uniform that he designed for them over a thousand years ago. They were very friendly and we took pictures with them. I didn't think they could do much to defend the Pontiff against any type of invasion with only those swords they were sporting. Every twelve feet or so, there was a man dressed in a navy blue suit and tie with a white shirt. They're known as the Pope's gentlemen. They keep the peace; tell you where to go and how to behave. If you are not dressed modestly enough they make you buy a scarf to tie around your shoulders or your waist. They reminded the crowd they were in a holy place and behavior must reflect it.

After what seemed like a two hour wait, we were ushered into a large air conditioned building and told to take seats. Vatican police, Pope's Gentlemen and Swiss Guards were everywhere. Anyone who even looked like they might try to act out was quickly subdued. I had a seat in the front row of the last group of what looked to be more than a thousand or so chairs. A small band of young excited women entered. They were standing right in front of me chattering in their native tongue. They were stepping all over me and others in that row. Within minutes the police were there, made them move off and find seats elsewhere. Elizabeth had been to an audience with the Pope before so she was sitting a few rows back. I looked her way and mouthed "When will we get to see him?" She came forward and said that this was so unusual compared with other audiences she had attended. "First of all it is not usually indoors like this in nice weather," she said as a roar from the crowd went up. The Pope passed by in magnificent splendor riding in the little Pope Mobile. He was waving at everyone. He was guided to the front of the building and driven up onto a big stage. He was helped to a large thrown-like chair and a microphone. We were led in prayer. Then his bishops and close ally began to recognize different groups in attendance from all over the world. I was totally taken with the Pontiff at that point. Without missing a beat, he spoke to each group in their own native tongue easily and effortlessly going from one language to another without the slightest bit of difficulty. I was really impressed. I could see on the monitor that he was reading from a prepared format, however, I knew how hard I struggled to speak going from English to Italian or Spanish. It was a miracle that should have brought people to their knees. I wondered why there wasn't more respect for him and the elderly who lived and learned so much. One day they will be gone and all their knowledge buried with them and forgotten. I knew then my whole journey and struggle through a very hard life was more than worth its weight in gold. Seeing Italy and Sicily had helped me learn much about my ancestry and about myself. I knew that my love and respect for the elderly was not lost on them but a real gift fromGod.

Chapter 18

Rocking Chairs, Rocking Cradles

Someone once said "Old age is not for the weak and meek. You have to be tough if you are going to live to become old." When we are young, we don't think we will ever be that old person we see at the grocery, in the park or on a bus. When my friend and long-time coworker, Sister Eleanor, was unable to take care of herself or live alone, she was taken to the Mother House of her order. "I don't want to be there with all these old women!" she protested loudly to me the day she got the news. I looked at her and noted her white hair and bent shoulders. Although her memory was failing, I still couldn't beat her in a game of checkers. Some things never get old. The things we learn in childhood stay with us forever. Respect and caring for the elderly should be taught in childhood. If it is never taught, it is never learned later in life. It remains the best way to ensure that the golden years will be golden instead of brown and lonely.

Caring for the elderly is never easy. When I look back on the years I cared for my mother, when she didn't even know who I was, I realize that I would give anything to have her back for just one more day. Once a loved one is gone, they are gone forever from this life. We can only hope we will be seeing them again in the hereafter. It is truly only a hope and trust that we will see them again after we die. No one has ever come back from the dead to tell us what it is like. So we must conclude that it is fine and wonderful because no one returns to complain. When friends and colleagues complain about their elderly relations, I remind them that soon they will not be here at all. I encourage them to enjoy their loved ones while they are still here. Be prepared for we know not the hour we are called from this earth.

Upon returning from Italy, I discovered that a friend, Barbara, whom I had worked with in hospital for many years, had her whole life stripped from her in a matter of months. I hadn't heard from her in a long while which wasn't unusual. If I left her a message at her home she shared with her mother, it would be months, but she would eventually call me back. The last time I phoned her, I left a threat instead of my usual call me back plea. When she replied, I was stunned to learn of her plight. The home they had insisted on staying in was in a rundown, gang infested neighborhood. It had been vandalized twenty times in the last eight months. Every time they went away from the house for any length of time the home had been broken into and was eventually rendered unlivable. The local authorities were unable or unwilling to catch the perpetrators. Barbara and her mother had been living at an extended stay motel in a safer area. Her mother had suffered a devastating stroke. The prospect of any type of restorative therapy was slim to none. Barbara faced putting her into a nursing home for custodial care.

Meanwhile, the building that was the church they had attended all of their lives was sold and would close soon. The church, that had seen them through good times and bad, would soon cease to exist. Life, as they knew it, for Barbara and her ailing mother was about to become totally non-existent. What do you say to someone who has lost so much? She had been a good nurse. She had never married, always opting to be chief cook and care taker of her parents. When Barbara suffered a serious heart attack, had to undergo open heart surgery, a pacemaker and automatic implanted defibrillator device implantation, her nursing career was ended. She had to go on disability. For a while, she and her mother were able to live comfortably on their respective social security. Her siblings had left the nest long ago making lives and homes for themselves in other parts of the world. Barbara had to figure things out alone.

When Medicare stopped paying for the rehabilitation center her mother was in, she was forced to find a facility to care for her. Barbara must pay the bill until all her mother's money would be gone. The only thing I could do for them was give Barbara a place to live while she figured things out. It is hard to believe, in a land so rich with resources, people who live so close by can be in such desperate peril. I don't believe anyone wants to face the fact that we could be, at any time in our lives, just like Barbara and her mother. Barbara's story was a sad commentary on life, but a teachable moment to young people. If you are wealthy, you will have everything. If you have some money it will be stripped from you until you are destitute and then the government will care for you. They will give the very least they can to accomplish it. Should you die while waiting for their help, then that's better still.

My neighbors who lived on the first floor of our building were a wonderful elderly couple. They had raised three daughters before coming to live in these beautiful surroundings. Benton finally retired after a long career as a jeweler and sold his store after more than fifty years. He passed away in his sleep one day a short time after his ninetieth birthday. His wife Sally began to fail after his death. She had always been the sick one. Their middle daughter, Grace, had assumed care for her mother and had hired a live-in care giver. The woman spoke no English. I felt she was very rude to Sally most of the time. After two years of around the clock care, Grace had exhausted almost all of Sally's savings. She and her husband moved Sally in with them and sold her condo. She continued to do well living with Grace but I could see it wasn't easy for either of them. The care giver still comes twice a week so Grace can go out and shop, run errands, visit and do some banking. If Grace was not a well and willing daughter, the fate of Sally would have been just another devastating story.

Even a well planned retirement can fall apart if you live longer than your resources will allow. I believe the answer lies in how we take care of one another or don't take care of one another. How we care for our children is how they will care for us one day. How we care for our parents is how our children will learn to care for us. It has been said that there is no greater love than to lay down your life for a friend. While we may not have to go that far, we surely can offer a helping hand to someone in need as it costs us little to be kind and thoughtful toward others.

When we are getting on with the business of life we need to consider these things. Most don't really, our aging, or infirmity much thought until it is too late to do much about it. We don't plan to live when we are going through life at top speed. We plan to work until we die. It was my thought all those years of working two and three jobs at a time. When I reached sixty-six I realized I no longer had the stamina or drive to work every day from sun up till sun down.

Kids and old people need so little to make them happy. It is the time we spend with them that they want and need the most. Sally thrived in her daughter's home. When I visited her for lunch, she insisted Grace put out the best china, Waterford crystal and the good silver. I felt like the Queen of England going there for high tea. For the elderly, one day can blend into the next without definition if it were not for little get-togethers every now and then.

I have known some elderly who just have so much energy and fortitude despite their advancing years. They seem to be able to do things for others and carry on a life style at a pace that seems tiring even to someone like me. My friend, Hannah, who is in her nineties, has endured so much in her life time. She has out lived two husbands, both of whom were physicians. Her one and only daughter married late in life. She had a difficult time getting pregnant and having children. It was a joyous time for her when she became pregnant with twins, however, only one of them survived. When the baby was seven months old, she discovered breast cancer that had gone undetected and had spread to the bones. She lost her battle with this terrible disease when her son was five years old. My friend Hannah has had to be mother to the boy ever since. He is fourteen now and she worries she won't live long enough to see him through to adulthood.

The boy was born with many birth defects and has had multiple corrective surgeries. Perhaps the mother never realized how seriously impaired her own health was at that time. Every time the boy needs another surgery, my friend goes into a tail spin worrying over him. She spends a lot of time with him, taking the boy and his friends wherever they wish to go. They go to the movies, the pool hall or to the arcade in the mall. She takes them out for fast food. She has seen all of the awful monster movies and listens to ear splitting rock, rap, and hip hop music. I am truly amazed by her every day. She doesn't want the boy to be alone when he gets home from school because his father works late into the evening. On weekends, when the father is out of town, my friend, Hannah, will spend the whole of that time with him. The fortitude of my friend, well into her ninety, is an eighth wonder of the world.

I believe my own mother lived just to care for an older brother of mine who was still living at home well into his sixty's. I think she finally gave into death when she realized that she could no longer do heavy laundry and go up and down stairs. She couldn't remember when she put pots on the stove until they were burning. Slowing, my brother began to assume some of these duties. She became weaker and less alert after that until she joined my father in the hereafter.

The baby boomer generation has become today's senior citizens. While I am not among this group, as I'm older by a year or two, I see they approach old age much differently than the previous generation. The new old folks are more active and many don't or can't plan to retire. They didn't have the opportunity to save and plan for the future or they just didn't get around to it. Many of them are raising their grandchildren in the role of still being parents. Many have adult children who are still living at home because they can't get jobs or do not make enough income to live on their own. Extended family homes are becoming the norm rather than the exception. It could be a positive change as it may decrease the need for nursing homes for the elderly. Many families choose to keep the elderly in their home because they depend on that family member's retirement income. It is a hardship on the entire family when that elderly person must seek a level of health care that can't be met at home. The income of the elderly parent then goes to the institution providing that care.

The coming together of the family just may be the silver lining during a terrible economy. While the young are struggling with this new depression, which is a depression much like the one my parents and most grandparents endured during the thirty's. The elderly are doing ok in it. They have social security and Medicare. The bad part of the present economy is that it is making the rich richer and the poor poorer. It is almost wiping out the middle class. Most of them are just that, caught in the middle of this crisis with no way to get out.

It is amazing to me that almost none of the problems and policy concerns that are dominating the twenty-four hour a day news cycle have impacted people in my age bracket. It has not affected the ones that are well and can take care of themselves. My generation has paid into Medicare and social security for all our lives and we are now reaping the benefits of having done so. It is the next generation who will not be as fortunate. There are more people who can't or no longer have to pay into the system. We have less people here in the USA paying into the system than we did fifty years ago when I started my career. We haven't the jobs, resources, or young skilled and unskilled labor to sustain the number of people who are turning age Sixty-five every day. It is one of the reasons why our pay-it-forward programs are suffering. Also the Medicare Cap is a problem. If a person makes more than one hundred eighteen thousand per year, after that first one hundred eighteen thousand of earnings they no longer have to pay into it. It continues to amaze me, those who do not pay into the system are the ones controlling it and telling those who do pay that they can't have it! We continue to spend more of the budget every year on defense than any other government program. More than two-thirds of all government spending, to be exact, goes for defense and the military. Less than a fourth goes into social programs, Medicare, Medicaid and Social Security. It is a reality lost on most Americans who listen to TV and radio as they constantly report that these programs are draining the federal budget. Nothing can be farther from the truth. This type of fear mongering drives the economy more than any other factor. It is more powerful than the threat of terrorism or war. The reason such terror can be fed to the masses every day, in a country so far advanced with such an elaborate communication system, is that there is a definite disconnect between the past, present and future in our young people. If you were to ask any of them about history, they know nothing of it and hardly know what happened twenty years ago let alone one hundred years ago. It is a major problem in our society today. I was always fascinated by that segment of the Jay Leno show when he goes out and asks ordinary Americans simple questions on history or even recent events. Most had no clue what his was talking about. They were unable to identify some of the most famous photos of people and places.

The faults of this disconnect with past, present and future lies with the education system. The system has clearly failed the young. I'm not sure what's being taught in schools these days but I am sure it is not history or current events. These were things of priority in my day. I understand now they take a back seat to computer science and the musical sound known as hip hop. I'm not saying these things are bad or unimportant; I just think the young need to know from where and how they came to be in the first place. We need to know and understand our history in order to understand our present and our future on this planet. In order to live better and advance into the future, the very young and the very old need to know each other well. Society needs to promote such a connection. Therefore, having grandma and grandpa under one roof with the rest of the family may serve such a purpose. The elderly will get the love and care they need. The young will learn of the past and how important it is to their future.

The next time you're in the grocery store and an old lady runs over your feet with her shopping cart as she cuts in front of you in the check-out line, please don't get angry. Do not curse all old people under your breath, do something different. Step back and talk to her. Ask her how she is today and if you might be of some assistance. You may learn something important about her, about history and about yourself in the process. I recall riding the train with my daughter, one day many years ago, when she was just a small girl. We were going into the Big City to shop and see Santa. An elderly lady cut in front of my daughter and grabbed the first seat in the train car. It was the very one we were headed for so we would have a good view on the ride into the city. "Mommy, she took our seat!" my daughter said loudly.

"It's ok, Honey. We can sit in the one across from her and we will be riding backwards. We can see where we've been instead of where we are going. It will be fun." I replied as calmly as I could, I was irritated myself. When we were seated, oblivious to what she had done, the woman smiled at me and said "Hello" as if she knew me. I looked at her in earnest. I realized that I did, indeed, know the woman. I had attended her during an illness when she needed home nursing. I often moon lighted with an agency for extra cash.

"Why, Hello Mrs. Evington. How are you? It's good to see you well, out and about." I replied.

"It's good to be going down town. I have to do some banking and a little shopping. I only have my house keeper and companion Julia. My husband and I had no children." She looked at my daughter and smiled. "You are so fortunate to have children. We were always busy people, my husband and I. He was an attorney you know. He worked for the great Clarence Darrow. He worked very hard and we lived well but what I wouldn't give now for a grandchild or two." I had heard of Mr. Darrow. I knew little of him but later that night when the children were in bed, I looked into the encyclopedia for information about him. I learned he was a great American criminal lawyer and social activist. As I read up on the great American, I realized I had been in the presence of someone who knew great history first hand. I appreciated her all the more for her sharing some of it with me and my daughter.

We lived in the city when my children were small. I recall meeting one of my neighbors who lived on the same block. She was elderly and didn't get out much. I learned that she was the granddaughter of the man who started one of the oldest beer companies in the USA. I knew that brand of beer because I could remember my father liked it best after a hard day in the hot summer sun. She had been living alone, abandoned, perhaps, by whatever relatives she had left. I'm sure she could have shared lots of family history with them had any of them cared enough to listen. It was lost to them forever when the last of that old generation died.

I have always been fascinated with people who have done great things. Even as a small child while living on the farm, I can remember walking down the street in our small town and seeing Winnie Rockefeller chasing after her son who was about my age at the time. I was holding my father's hand as she zoomed by us. She called out a greeting to him. People stopped and said "There goes Winnie Rockefeller. I don't know why she insists on returning to our one horse town". Winnie was a local girl who had married into the Rockefeller family at a very young age. I didn't know, at that time, that the name Rockefeller had any great significance. But I never forgot that woman who was quite tall and beautiful. I never forgot that she was from a famous family, yet she had the grace to greet everyone that day on the street while chasing her rowdy boy. I guess you can take the girl out of the small town but you can't take the small town out of the girl.

One of the greatest advantages of growing old is you can sit and gaze out your window and recall these little incidences that happened so long ago with such vivid recollection. You can see it anew with your old eyes as if you are seeing it play out in a Technicolor movie. Life can be a movie that runs continuously in every old person's memory as we age. It is one of the great gifts of old age. I can write about the past as if it happened yesterday.

I find I can write much better on a sunny day than a gray one. It seems to make the remembering so much easier. Today is such a day, bright and shining with green grass and a gentle breeze over the golf course outside my window. This is strange weather once again for winter. I have Christmas music on the radio and outside my window it looks like a perfect spring day. Although the whole climate change thing is very scary, it does, at times, bring some of the best weather I have ever seen in my life time. It is just too bad that it also brings the opposite in other parts of the country. While we here in the Midwest are enjoying these mild days, the poor folks on the east coast are suffering some of the worst devastation our nation has ever seen. A hurricane that came ashore a few weeks ago had pounded the coast. It is quite bizarre to witness such a phenomena occurring before our very eyes. We just have to trust that God knows His plan which we may never know or come to understand in our life time. We just have to stop and thank Him sometimes for the beauty of the Earth even when we know not when it will turn on us. One thing is for certain life is so strange.

If one day you find yourself in the company of an elderly person, try to get them to tell you their story. Those who rock chairs, most likely, once rocked cradles. They have a wealth of knowledge they could share with the rest of us. It may bring life in the present into some kind of perspective.

It seems I've spent the whole of my life running against the wind. But I know, on those rare occasions, when the wind turns in your favor, then life is all the sweeter and worth every bit of the struggle.

Acknowledgement

A heart felt thank you to all my friends and family who have journeyed with me while I have written my life story. This book is the last of my three memoirs but, I hope not the last book I will write. Thank You Alice Hopper and Toni K. Anderson for your help and kind patience with me. I know I can be demanding. I thank God for my ability to write and remember. I thank Him for the elderly in my life who have helped me and given me rich recollections to reflect upon in my writings. I thank my daughters for being mine in my life. I don't know what my life would have been without them. Thank You to my great niece April Marie Matury for creating yet another beautiful cover for my third memoir.

The names and places in this book have all been changed; however, all the stories are true as I remember them. Any resemblance is purely coincidental.

In Mary E. Gibson's third volume of her memoirs, "Against the Wind," she draws her readers from the curtains of hospital politics to the dark, hidden corridors of nursing rehabilitation facilities. While portraying the stark conditions at the various facilities to which she is assigned in her role as nurse practitioner, a profession she defines in detail, she describes her typical work days. Amidst the foul stenches, gory observations and disturbing conversations, Mary walks readers through her arduous rounds of treating her patients at five different nursing homes. During her grueling 12-hour days, she treats 20-30 patients who require her constant attention and care, before assuming her on-call duties of responding to at least a half a dozen emergency phone calls. Most nights, she gets only a few hours of sleep.

Caught between the facility owners' profit motives, strict legal regulations, managed care, decreased public funding and the frequent incompetence of many facility staff members, she expresses her ongoing sense of feeling powerless to truly help the very people she is committed to serve. The hope of imminent retirement and the nightly comic relief she gets from watching Jay Leno help to keep her going through her day-to-day grind. In the spirit of her previous memoirs, Mary reveals her profound fortitude, perseverance, faith and inspiring optimism amidst her constant trials, including her own injuries and health problems. This is a must read for everyone, especially for baby boomers who may soon be facing their own needs for nursing and rehabilitation care.

Jack Murray
Retired Editor of The Regional News Freelance Writer

CPSIA information can be obtained
at www.ICGtesting.com
Printed in the USA
FSHW020156140820
72935FS

9 781648 950384